Dilip Mehta

First published 1986 by Collins Publishers, New York, London, Glasgow, Toronto, Sydney, Auckland, Johannesburg.

Library of Congress Cataloging-in-Publication Data
Main entry under title: A Day in the Life of America

ISBN 0-00-217734-X

1. United States—Description and travel—1981—Views. 2. United States—Social life and customs—1971—Pictorial works. 3. Photography, Journalistic—United States.
I. Smolan, Rick.
II. Cohen, David.

E169.04.D38 1986
973.927'022'2 86-17190

Project Directors: Rick Smolan and David Cohen

Art Director: Leslie Smolan

Printed in Japan First printing August 1986

10 9 8 7 6 5 4 3 2 1

A Day in the Life of America

Photographed by 200 of the world's leading photojournalists on one day, May 2, 1986

The Sand Hills of Nebraska, 6:30 a.m.: Five-year-old Merici Vinton sleeps securely in her parents' bed.

Richard Olsenius

Charleston, South Carolina, 6:30 a.m.: The Citadel's
2,000 cadets wake up to a bugler blowing
reveille over the school's public-address system.

Aaron Chang

Graciela Iturbide

East Los Angeles, California, 7 a.m.: A young Mexican-American woman named Rosario plays with her five-month-old son Joe.

Battle Creek, Michigan, 7:30 a.m.: Sandra Carver, 18, gears up for her final month of classes at Lakeview High School. She says she can't clean up her room because she's too busy studying for final exams.

Eric Lars Bakke

Galen Rowell

The book you are holding in your hands is a visual time capsule, an impression of life in America taken on Friday, May 2, 1986, by 200 of the world's leading photographers. No picture here is more than twenty-four hours older or younger than any other, and no picture here has been shot for any purpose other than to document the harmonies and paradoxes of life in America as it was lived on this one ordinary day.

America is a complex country and a proud one. It is an idea, a beckoning, an opportunity. It has always been an improbable country, and to set out to capture it in a single day was an improbable, some would say, impossible, idea.

A Day in the Life of America does not claim to be the true record of even one day. A day cannot be collected as it passes by in a blaze of light between shadows. Yet on May 2nd America yielded some of its secrets to these world class photographers. There are several hundred photographs here, culled from more than 235,000. But even 235,000 images barely hint at the infinite moments that passed through the hills and homes and hearts of America on that day. On May 2nd America was frozen in time and, for decades to come, our children and our children's children will look at these pages with wonder at a day when 200 photographers made time stand still.

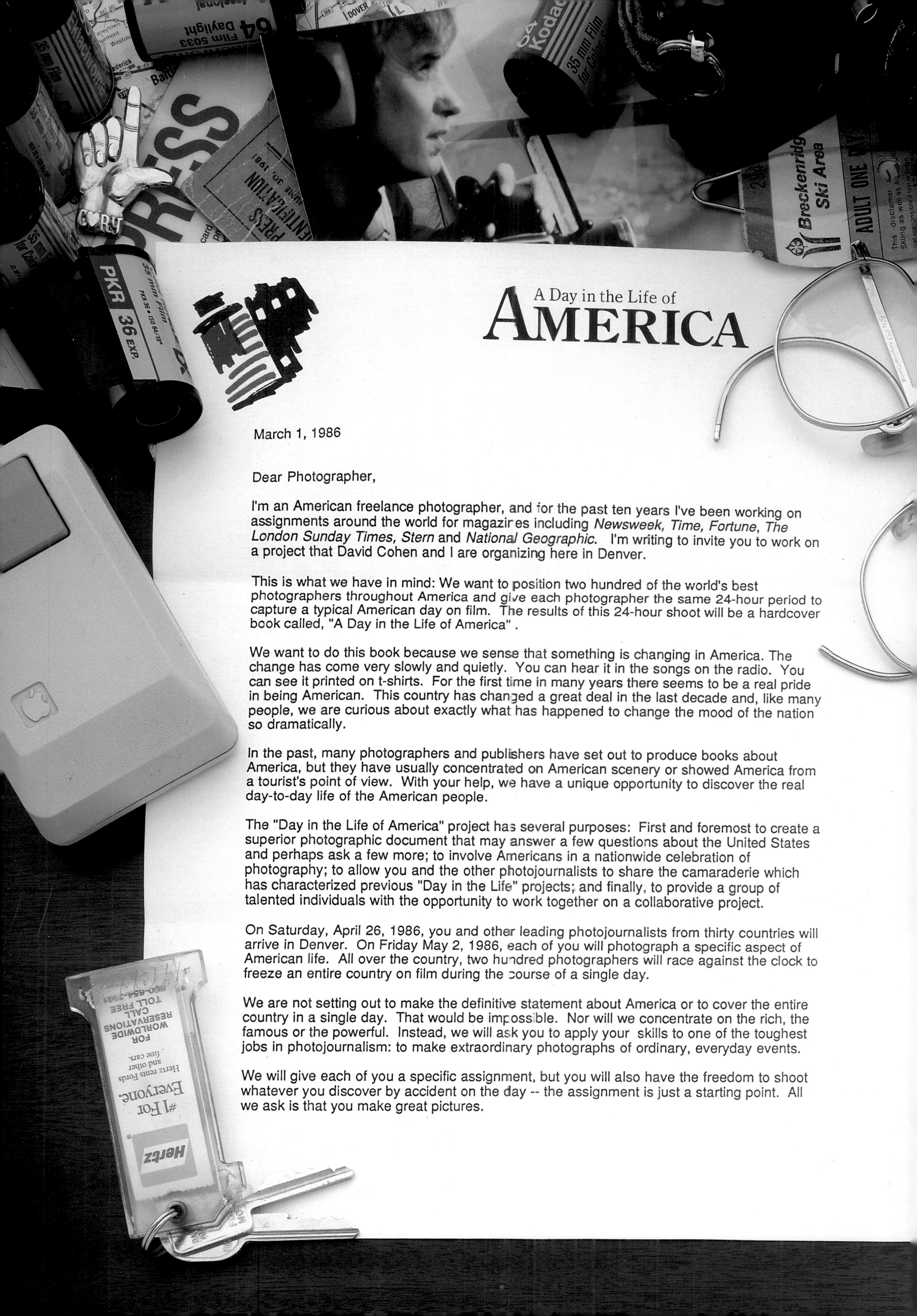

A Day in the Life of
AMERICA

March 1, 1986

Dear Photographer,

I'm an American freelance photographer, and for the past ten years I've been working on assignments around the world for magazines including *Newsweek, Time, Fortune, The London Sunday Times, Stern* and *National Geographic*. I'm writing to invite you to work on a project that David Cohen and I are organizing here in Denver.

This is what we have in mind: We want to position two hundred of the world's best photographers throughout America and give each photographer the same 24-hour period to capture a typical American day on film. The results of this 24-hour shoot will be a hardcover book called, "A Day in the Life of America" .

We want to do this book because we sense that something is changing in America. The change has come very slowly and quietly. You can hear it in the songs on the radio. You can see it printed on t-shirts. For the first time in many years there seems to be a real pride in being American. This country has changed a great deal in the last decade and, like many people, we are curious about exactly what has happened to change the mood of the nation so dramatically.

In the past, many photographers and publishers have set out to produce books about America, but they have usually concentrated on American scenery or showed America from a tourist's point of view. With your help, we have a unique opportunity to discover the real day-to-day life of the American people.

The "Day in the Life of America" project has several purposes: First and foremost to create a superior photographic document that may answer a few questions about the United States and perhaps ask a few more; to involve Americans in a nationwide celebration of photography; to allow you and the other photojournalists to share the camaraderie which has characterized previous "Day in the Life" projects; and finally, to provide a group of talented individuals with the opportunity to work together on a collaborative project.

On Saturday, April 26, 1986, you and other leading photojournalists from thirty countries will arrive in Denver. On Friday May 2, 1986, each of you will photograph a specific aspect of American life. All over the country, two hundred photographers will race against the clock to freeze an entire country on film during the course of a single day.

We are not setting out to make the definitive statement about America or to cover the entire country in a single day. That would be impossible. Nor will we concentrate on the rich, the famous or the powerful. Instead, we will ask you to apply your skills to one of the toughest jobs in photojournalism: to make extraordinary photographs of ordinary, everyday events.

We will give each of you a specific assignment, but you will also have the freedom to shoot whatever you discover by accident on the day -- the assignment is just a starting point. All we ask is that you make great pictures.

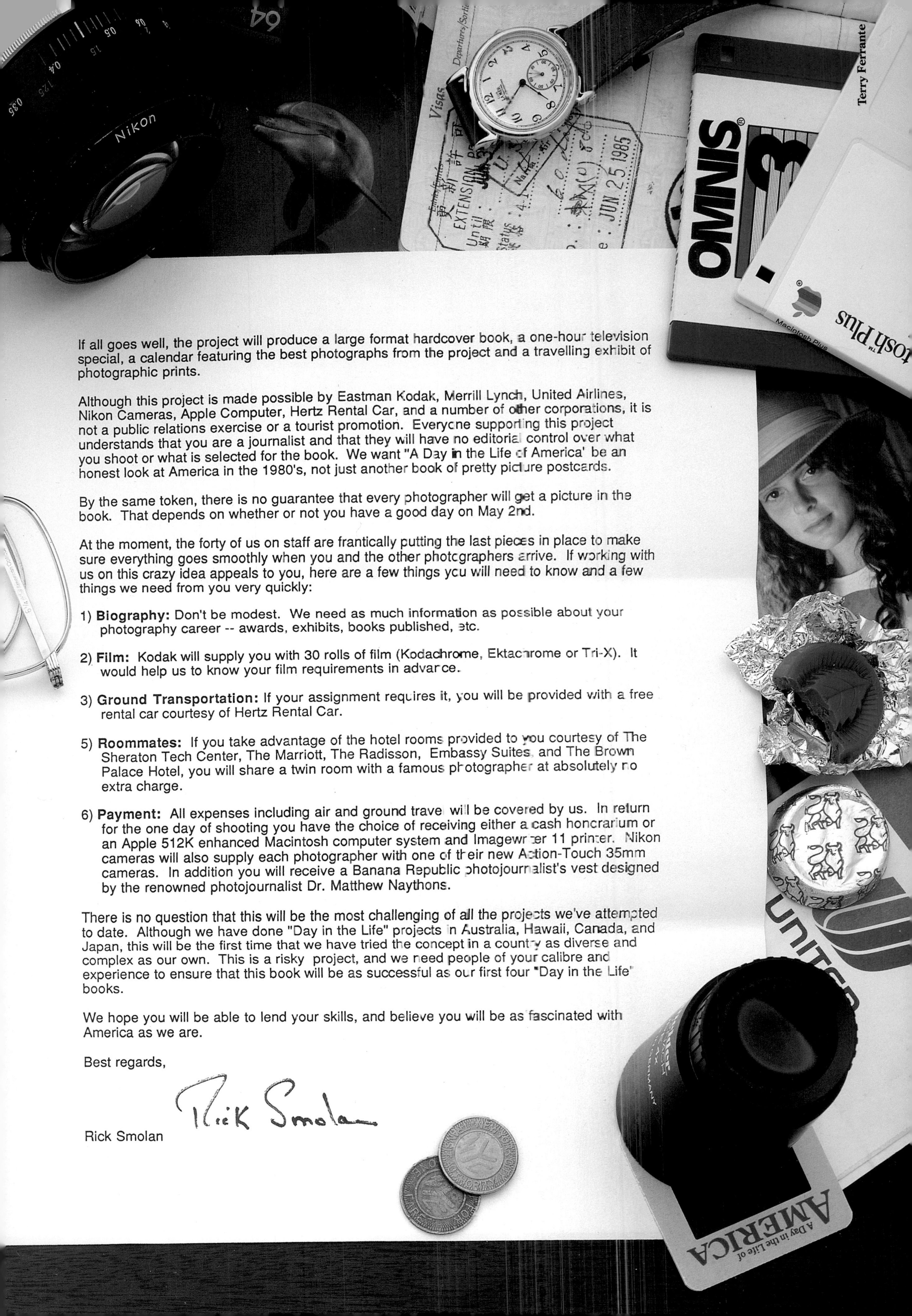

If all goes well, the project will produce a large format hardcover book, a one-hour television special, a calendar featuring the best photographs from the project and a travelling exhibit of photographic prints.

Although this project is made possible by Eastman Kodak, Merrill Lynch, United Airlines, Nikon Cameras, Apple Computer, Hertz Rental Car, and a number of other corporations, it is not a public relations exercise or a tourist promotion. Everyone supporting this project understands that you are a journalist and that they will have no editorial control over what you shoot or what is selected for the book. We want "A Day in the Life of America' be an honest look at America in the 1980's, not just another book of pretty picture postcards.

By the same token, there is no guarantee that every photographer will get a picture in the book. That depends on whether or not you have a good day on May 2nd.

At the moment, the forty of us on staff are frantically putting the last pieces in place to make sure everything goes smoothly when you and the other photographers arrive. If working with us on this crazy idea appeals to you, here are a few things you will need to know and a few things we need from you very quickly:

1) **Biography:** Don't be modest. We need as much information as possible about your photography career -- awards, exhibits, books published, etc.

2) **Film:** Kodak will supply you with 30 rolls of film (Kodachrome, Ektachrome or Tri-X). It would help us to know your film requirements in advance.

3) **Ground Transportation:** If your assignment requires it, you will be provided with a free rental car courtesy of Hertz Rental Car.

5) **Roommates:** If you take advantage of the hotel rooms provided to you courtesy of The Sheraton Tech Center, The Marriott, The Radisson, Embassy Suites, and The Brown Palace Hotel, you will share a twin room with a famous photographer at absolutely no extra charge.

6) **Payment:** All expenses including air and ground travel will be covered by us. In return for the one day of shooting you have the choice of receiving either a cash honorarium or an Apple 512K enhanced Macintosh computer system and Imagewriter 11 printer. Nikon cameras will also supply each photographer with one of their new Action-Touch 35mm cameras. In addition you will receive a Banana Republic photojournalist's vest designed by the renowned photojournalist Dr. Matthew Naythons.

There is no question that this will be the most challenging of all the projects we've attempted to date. Although we have done "Day in the Life" projects in Australia, Hawaii, Canada, and Japan, this will be the first time that we have tried the concept in a country as diverse and complex as our own. This is a risky project, and we need people of your calibre and experience to ensure that this book will be as successful as our first four "Day in the Life" books.

We hope you will be able to lend your skills, and believe you will be as fascinated with America as we are.

Best regards,

Rick Smolan

Rick Smolan

RAVINE TRAIL

Climbing instructor Joseph Lentini faces 80-mile-per-hour winds and a minus 40 degree wind-chill factor as he starts a four-mile walk down Lionshead Trail from the weather station at the summit of New Hampshire's Mount Washington.

Pulitzer Prize-winning photographer Jay Dickman of Dallas, Texas, reports that five minutes after he stepped outside the weather station, every one of his cameras had completely iced over. It took Dickman two hours to take his cameras apart and de-ice them. He then wrapped all of his equipment in plastic bags, went back outside and only unwrapped each camera long enough to take a picture. Dickman says, "I'd always heard about this mountain and how dangerous it's supposed to be in the winter. Now I can see why over a hundred people have been killed up there."

Photographer:
Jay Dickman, USA

● *Previous page*

8:45 AM

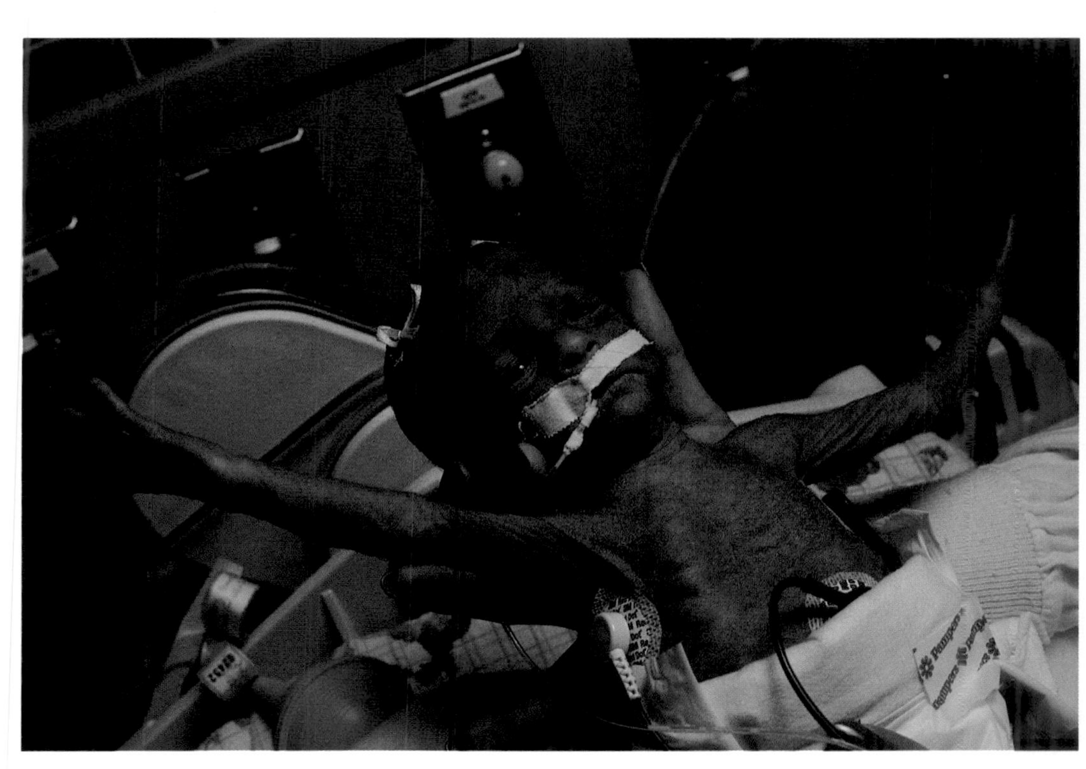

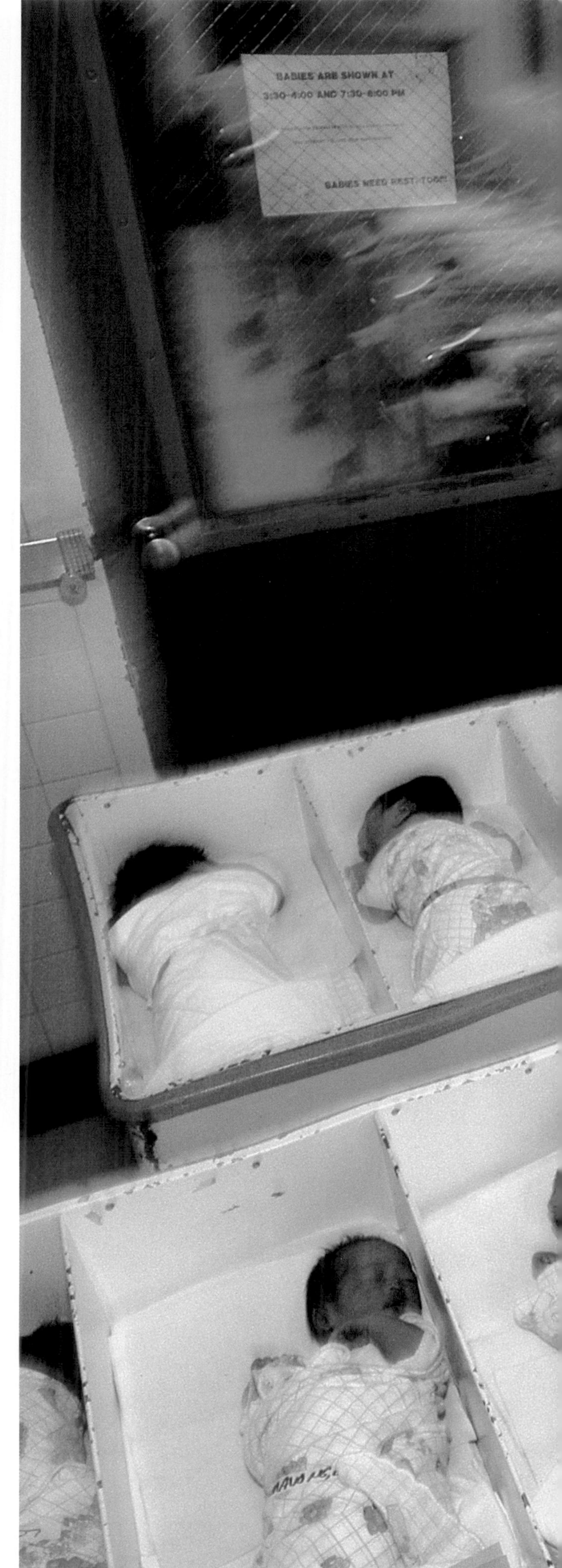

● *Above, top*

Tracy Martinez was born eight weeks premature at Dallas' Parkland Memorial Hospital. At the time of birth, Tracy weighed only 2 lbs., 12 ozs. and was 15 inches long. A week later, on May 2nd, Tracy's lungs were still too undeveloped to breathe unaided, and she was taking oxygen and formula through tubes.

Photographer:
Barry Lewis, Britain

● *Above*

After leading a ten-member surgical team through a seven-and-a-half-hour artificial heart implant and a six-hour heart and lung transplant, Dr. Bartley P. Griffith falls asleep in the surgeons' lounge at Presbyterian-University Hospital in Pittsburgh. Dr. Griffith's team has performed over 35 heart-lung transplants, helping to make Pittsburgh one of the organ transplant capitals of the world.

Photographer:
Serge Cohen, France

● *Right*

Newborn babies are carted through Parkland Memorial Hospital in Dallas four times a day to visit their parents. On average one baby is born every half hour at Parkland, the third highest birthrate of any hospital in the country.

Photographer:
Barry Lewis, Britain

Following page

Lighter-than-air enthusiasts from across the Pacific Northwest take off in Walla Walla, Washington, during the 1986 Balloon Stampede. Most of the pack returned to earth an hour later five miles away. A typical hot-air rig costs about $20,000.

Photographer:
Steve Ringman, USA

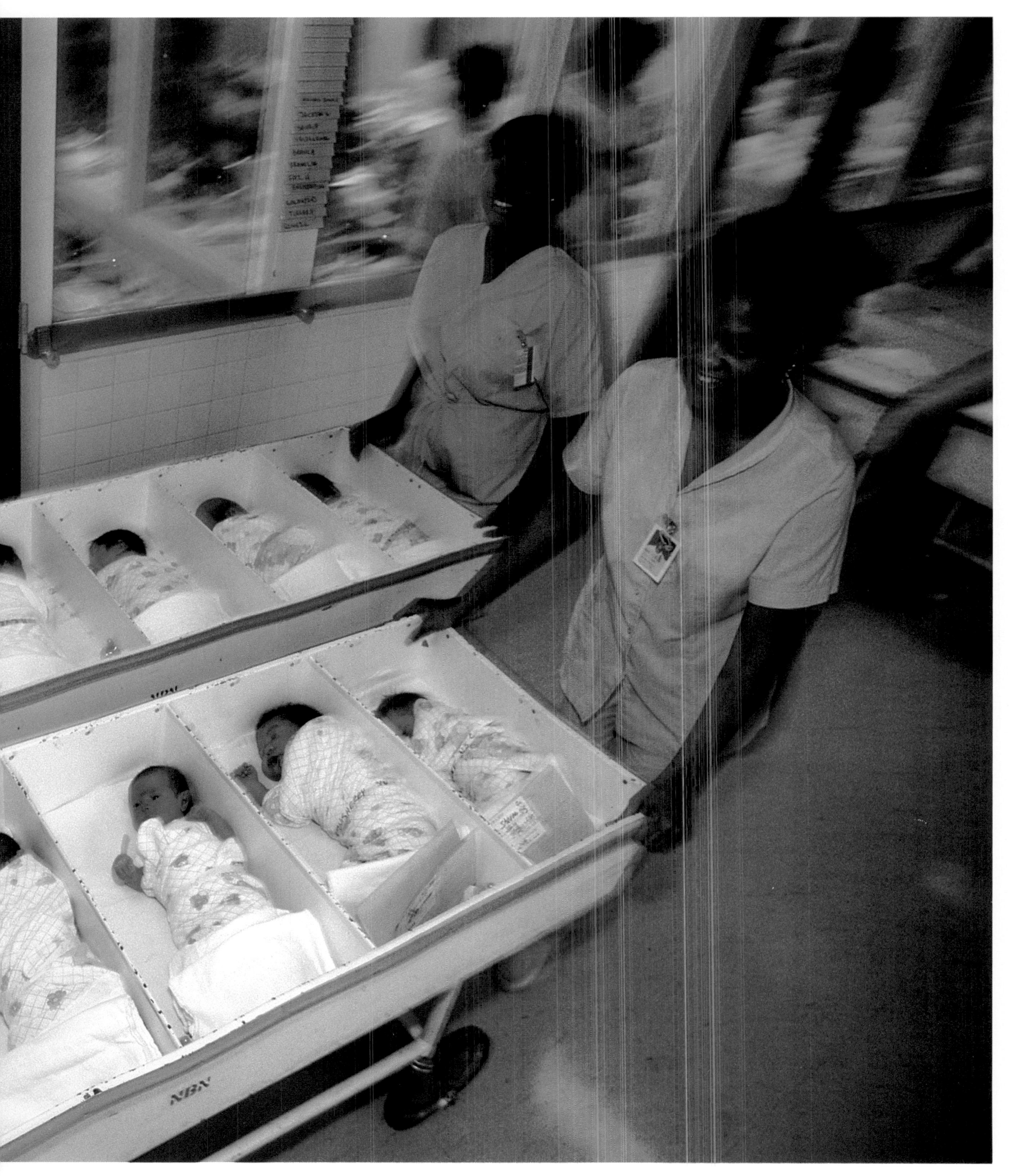

Steve Ringman

Spokane

Mexico City-based photographer Graciela Iturbide spent May 2nd with a group of East Los Angeles *cholos*—a loose term for the small fringe of tough, street-wise young Mexican-Americans, mostly U.S. born—who see themselves at odds with both Anglo society and Hispanic tradition. As Iturbide explains, her subjects—members of a *cholo* street gang—were unusual in another way:

"Arturo, Lisa, Rosario and five-month-old Joe live together in the White Fence *barrio* of East L.A. Except for the baby, all are deaf-mutes. Joe is Rosario's baby, but since none of the group has a job now, they all take care of him. They spend a lot of time in their room together and driving around in their car with the baby looking for friends. Each has a nickname. Arturo is called 'Chango.' Lisa is 'Bad Girl,' and Rosario is 'Smiley.' Rosario calls her baby 'El Boo Boo.'

Photographer:
Graciela Iturbide, Mexico

9:45 AM

• *Below*

Why would anyone need an ultraviolet tanning bed in sun-drenched Albuquerque, New Mexico? "Because everyone works

• *Right*

Jenny Hope slides into a tub of volcanic mud at Nance's Hot Springs in Calistoga, California. The hot springs have been

10:00 AM

• *Above*

The Ciemniak family meat store has been serving up homemade *kielbasa* on Joseph Campau street in Hamtramck, Michigan, since 1921.

For generations, Polish immigrants have beaten a path to the inner-city Detroit enclave—and high-paying assembly-line jobs in the nearby auto plants. In recent years, however, many of their children and grandchildren have moved to the suburbs, and Hamtramck's newest arrivals include Yugoslavs, Czechs and other Eastern Europeans.

Photographer:

Dennis Chamberlin, USA

• *Right*

On May 2nd, waitress Emma Maison contends with some of the nearly 1,900 kosher breakfasts served to guests at the Concord Hotel in the Catskill Mountains. The Concord, a sprawling resort on the shores of Kiamesha Lake, caters mostly to Jewish families from the New York City area.

Photographer:

Victor Fisher, Canada

• *Following page*

In Boonville, Missouri, members of the Kemper Military School and College swim team line up in Johnston Field House. Kemper was founded in 1844, and its graduates first fought for the South during the War Between the States.

Photographer:

Nina Barnett, USA

WALK
WALK
DON'T RUN

Nina Barnett

● *Left*

Eileen Slocum lives year-round in a mansion built by her aunt, Georgette Brown, in 1894. Her home is one of the largest "cottages" in the old-line summer resort of Newport, Rhode Island. A direct descendent of Roger Williams, who founded the state in 1636, Mrs. Slocum and her husband, John, a retired diplomat, have 11 grandchildren. Her chef, Carlos Juarez, worked in the Washington embassy of his native Argentina until its ambassador was recalled during the 1982 Falkland Islands War.

Photographer:
Michael O'Brien, USA

● *Above*

In downtown Philadelphia's Reading Terminal Market, James Jackson offers a complete menu of shoe shines. The mural behind customers David O'Neil and Walt McCulla is modeled on John Trumbull's 18th-century painting that depicts the signing of the Declaration of Independence in nearby Independence Hall. Thanks to a carefully planned renovation, the sprawling Reading Terminal, once a fading commuter rail stop, has taken on a new shine of its own.

Photographer:
Patrick Ward, Britain

● *Following page*

Flesh and bones: On May 2nd, model Larry Gilkes was one of two possible subjects at an illustration class at New York City's Fashion Institute of Technology.

Photographer:
Burk Uzzle, USA

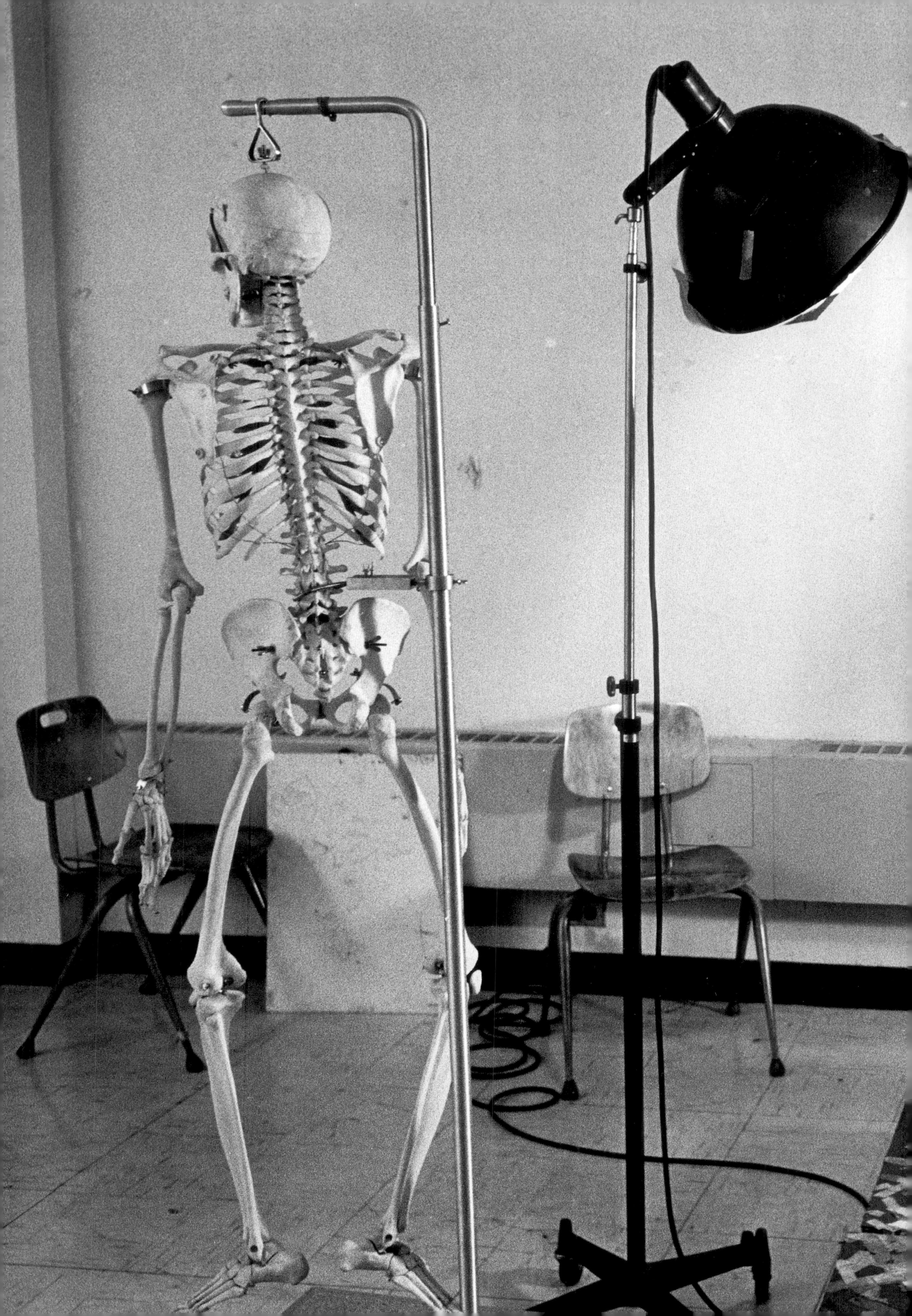

Burk Uzzle

• *Left*

It took sculptor Gutzon Borglum 14 years and a lot of dynamite to carve Mount Rushmore National Memorial into the granite of southwestern South Dakota. On May 2nd, photographer J. P. Laffont climbed up for a closer look at Thomas Jefferson and Abraham Lincoln.

Photographer:

Jean-Pierre Laffont, France

• *Above*

Guy and Margaret Holtzapple of York, Pennsylvania, enjoy the sun outside the Heritage Grand Hotel in Ft. Mill, South Carolina. Guy, a maintenance worker at York's Bonton department store, and Margaret, a machine operator, have been married for nearly 45 years.

Photographer:

Jerry Valente, USA

Odessa, Texas Andrew Stawicki

Juneau, Alaska Donna Ferrato

New York, New York Ralph Ginzberg

Cabin Creek, West Virginia

James L. Stanfiel

ew York, New York

Bill Pierce

Santa Fe, New Mexico

Arnaud de Wildenber

From the top of a manure pile at Hitch Feeders in Garden City, Kansas, a feedlot cowboy can survey 50,000 cattle having their last super-fattening supper before the final roundup. Trucked in from ranches across the country, the Angus, Hereford and Charlois steers chew their way through 370 tons of high-moisture Kansas feed corn each day.

Weighing in at around 700 pounds the day they walk in, the animals bulk up to nearly 1,100 pounds in just under four months. Then they are moved to holding pens (*following page*) at nearby Val-Agri Meat Packing Plant. An average of 2,800 cattle a day spend two or three hours in the pens before trundling off to the slaughterhouse, where they are stunned with high-voltage electricity, killed by a single bullet in the head and then carved up by teams of butchers using power saws. In 1985, Val-Agri, one of the country's top packers, shipped 831 million pounds of dressed beef—almost enough for one quarter-pound hamburger for every person on earth.

Photographer:
Chris Johns, USA

Chris Johns

● *Above*

Driving towards the Chisos Mountains in Big Bend National Park, Texas.
Photographer:
Tom Zetterstrom, USA

● *Right*

Cat owner Ginger Cantacessi posted a homemade warning to vehicles passing her Golden Valley, Nevada, home. Here she poses with Sylvia, one of her four cats.
Photographer:
Dana Fineman, USA

● *Following page*

The northbound Evanston Express waits to cross the Lake Street line in Chicago's downtown "Loop." The 215 miles of Chicago Transit Authority track—usually called the "el" for its many elevated sections—carries half a million riders daily.
Photographer:
Francoise Huguier, France

CAT
SLOW
CROSSING

Nashville, Tennessee

Tsuneo Enari, Japan

lew York, New York

Joy Wolf, USA

Chief Justice of the United States Warren E. Burger works on an opinion in his Supreme Court chambers in Washington, D.C.

Photographer Brian Lanker found the Chief Justice in a cooperative mood. Lanker says, "The Chief Justice was certainly conscious of his image, but he was relaxed enough to really work with me. He joked with my daughter, Jackie, who was assisting me, and I found him to be a very nice person. Gracious and, as everyone says, he certainly looks the role of the Chief Justice. People say the Supreme Court is a tough place to shoot, but I thought it was a breath of fresh air compared with the White House [*see following page*]."

The Chief Justice's light mood was surprising considering what he must have had on his mind. Less than a month after Lanker's session with America's 15th Chief Justice, Burger resigned his seat on the Court.

Photographer:
Brian Lanker, USA

CALCAGNO

A senior cadet at The Citadel in Charleston, South Carolina, pulled freshmen Paul Calcagno and Christopher Chope out of a morning line-up to demonstrate traditional "bracing." Says *Day in the Life of America* photographer Aaron Chang, "It's an extreme form of coming to attention that they make the freshmen do. They have to touch their shoulder blades together and bury their chins into their chests."

Chang, who is best known for his work as a surfing photographer, found it difficult to "infiltrate" a military academy. "I'm not really familiar with the military. I've never had any experience with them. What I had to do was win the trust of the cadets in a very short period of time. Relating to a military cadet is almost the opposite of relating to a surfer. It was really hard to get these guys to open up."

Photographer:
Aaron Chang, USA

In Louisiana's Cajun country, 64-year-old fisherman Louis Choplin heads out across Athchafalaya Swamp to look for crawfish. When Choplin first started trapping crawfish in 1928, 50 pounds went for 25 cents. These days, he gets $25 for the same amount.

In his long lifetime, Choplin has been a fisherman, a trapper, a soldier (he took part in the D-Day invasion of Normandy), a chef, a lumberjack, a butcher, a painter, a carpenter, a pipeline foreman and, yes, a volunteer Santa Claus at a local institute for the mentally retarded. Now, Choplin "lives in the swamp" with Gleanor, his wife of 41 years, and one of his four children. He crawfishes year-round and traps fur in the winter.

Photographer:
Matthew Naythons, USA

Robert Azzi

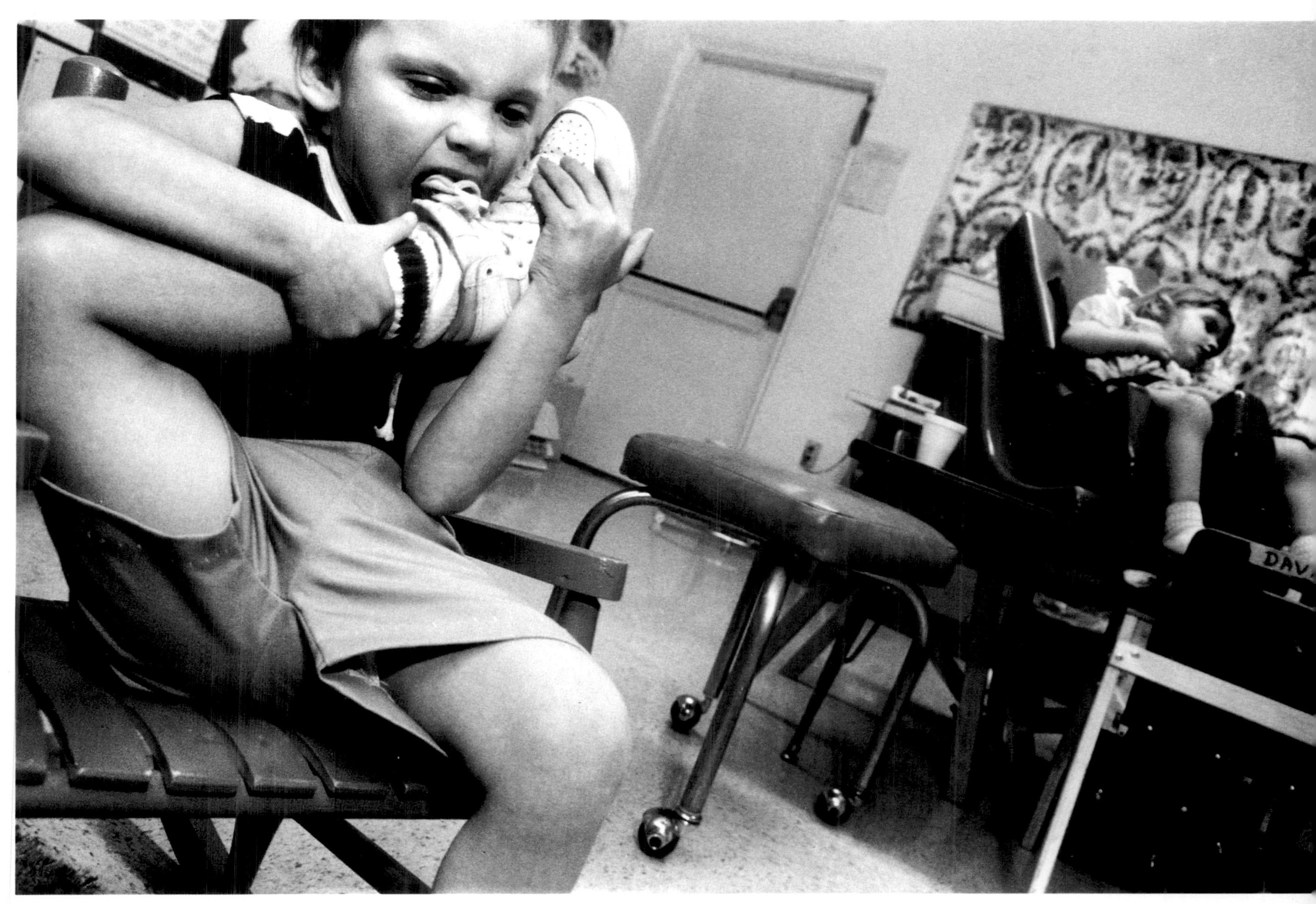

● *Previous page*

Temperate sea mists have nurtured this stand of *sequoia sempervirens* since Ghengis Khan started his march across Asia in the 13th century. The largest of these redwoods—located in 550-acre Muir Woods National Monument near San Francisco—top 250 feet in height and 13 feet in diameter.

Photographer:
Robert Azzi, USA

● *Above*

At the Upper Pinellas Association for Retarded Citizens (UPARC) training facility in Clearwater, Florida, five-year-old Patrick persists in using his teeth to untie his shoes. Normal at birth, he was blinded and severely brain-damaged by a high fever in 1985. In the background is three-year-old Michelle, one of seven other children in the group.

Photographer:
Mary Ellen Mark, USA

● *Right*

UPARC group home manager Anne Marvel helps 25-year-old Caren (who suffers from Down's syndrome) to get ready for a party at the residence. Marvel says, ''Caren can't arrange her hair and make-up herself, but when we're finished, she knows that she looks pretty, and she smiles. That makes my job here worthwhile. It's emotionally exhausting, but the rewards outweigh the frustrations, and at the end of the day I'm left with a good feeling inside.''

Photographer:
Mary Ellen Mark, USA

Saks Fifth Avenue

● *Left, top*

When southern California's hot spring sun became too oppressive, this Beverly Hills lady popped into Saks to buy a new sun hat

Photographer:
George Steinmetz, USA

● *Left, bottom*

There's almost always a waiting line for swimming pool blackjack at the Tropicana Hotel in Las Vegas, Nevada. In deference to the location, the tabletop is nylon instead of regulation green felt; a special heater behind the dealer dries out damp hundred-dollar bills.

Photographer:
Francois Robert, Switzerland

● *Below*

Water-exercise class meets three times a week in the pool at the Top of the World retirement community in Clearwater, Florida.

Photographer:
Mary Ellen Mark, USA

24-375 ML
MICH
WENATCHEE
CHIEF

• *Above*

Need a new—well, sort of—tail fin, engine or radio for your Piper Cub or Beechcraft? For 40 years, the J.W. Duff Aircraft Co. has been salvaging wrecked and obsolete planes at a ten-acre yard in Denver, Colorado.

Photographer:

Franco Zecchin, Italy

GUCCI

Left

Doorman Michael Canavan checks the time outside the Fifth Avenue branch of Gucci, internationally renowned purveyors of leather goods, handbags, fashions and accessories. The New York store's least expensive item, a Gucci keyring, costs $20. The dearest is an 18 carat Marquis cut canary diamond ring, available for a cool $345,000.
Photographer:
Jodi Cobb, USA

Left

Mary Cassell Johns Bernard considers a new evening outfit at Jack Krawcheck's for Women in her hometown of Charleston, South Carolina.
Photographer:
Aaron Chang, USA

Left

American designer Norma Kamali's fall '86 line debuts for the fashion press at her midtown boutique on West 56th Street in Manhattan.
Photographer:
Jodi Cobb, USA

Wilbur E. Garrett

• *Previous pages 102-103*

Laura Dickey, 77, and Charles Kenyon, 78, play bride and groom during the mock wedding portion of a senior citizen fashion show in Fairlee, Vermont. An unconfirmed rumor has it that, back in the 1920s, Miss Dickey had a little crush on Mr. Kenyon.

Photographer:
Christopher Pillitz, Britain

• *Previous page*

Robert Mondavi, one of America's best-known vintners, and his wife, Margrit Biever, like their privacy—which may explain why the couple's two-year-old, multimillion-dollar house in California's Napa Valley has an indoor swimming pool but only one bedroom.

Photographer:
Wilbur E. Garrett, USA

• *Above*

On May 2nd, Ronald Reagan was traveling in the Far East, but Vice President of the United States George Bush was on hand in the White House to welcome Cassie Camp Plunkett of Porum, Oklahoma, who celebrated her 100th birthday on March 15th.

Photographer:
Brian Lanker, USA

• *Right*

Photographer Vladimir Sichov left the U.S.S.R. in 1979, smuggling out 180,000 photographs—later widely published in the West—depicting hidden aspects of Soviet life. On May 2, 1986, near Rockefeller Center in midtown Manhattan, he found one of New York City's estimated 60,000 homeless men and women begging on a busy street corner. "I did those pictures in Russia," he says, "I do the same thing here."

Photographer:
Vladimir Sichov, Stateless

• *Following page*

Havana is 225 miles away, but daily lunch at her Uncle Antonio's is still an old-fashioned fam ily affair for Miami attorney Mar Elena Prio (center), a leading figure in the city's 700,000-strong Cuban community. Her late father, Carlos Prio Socarras was Cuba's last president befor dictator Fulgencio Batista took over in 1952.

Photographer:
Stephanie Maze, USA

Classic Bookshops
The Triumph of Politics
Why the Reagan Revolution Failed
David A. Stockman
I'M HUNGRY
PLEASE HELP

Stephanie Maze

250
300
150
150
150
275
325
100
100
125
GENUINE
Budweiser
THIS BUD'S FOR YOU.
GENUINE
KITCHEN CLOSES
MON - THURS 10.00
Fri. - SAT. P.M. 11.00
Brownies For Dessert
MENU
Fish Dinner $3.50
Fish & Salad $2.50
Taco Salad 2.00-2.50
Chef Salad 2.00-2.50

● *Left*

The Wagon Wheel Cafe is the center of small town life in Cuba, Kansas. The "menu" next to waitress Anna Kauer is a brownie which stayed in the oven a bit too long.

Photographer:
Jim Richardson, USA

● *Above*

William Banyard, age 20 months, is not quite sure about the driving conditions at Mike Pompa's barbershop, where most Greenwich, Connecticut, kids get their first haircut.

Photographer:
Nicole Bengiveno, USA

● *Left*

Yvonne Mitchell, 19, lives with her four-month-old son, Harry Simpson Jr., in North Lawndale, on Chicago's tough West Side. "There are some positive things happening in North Lawndale," says photographer Bruce Talamon. "I tried very hard to find them, but it was tough."

Photographer:
Bruce Talamon, USA

● *Above*

May 2nd was a big day for the Morgan family of Harlow, England. They were headed for a Hawaiian vacation aboard United Airlines Flight 1 out of Chicago.

Photographer Douglas Kirkland also had a big day. His assignment was to shoot America's first sunrise over Maine's Mount Katahdin (see page 1) and sunset the same day over Maui. He was halfway to Hawaii when he made this picture.

Photographer:
Douglas Kirkland, Canada

1:45 PM

• *Previous page*

Bill Angers is one of three window-washers who spend all of their working hours improving the view from the Hyatt Regency Hotel in downtown Dallas, Texas.
Photographer:
Barry Lewis, Britain

• *Above*

Window cleaner Danny Thomas and financial branch manager Robert Leacox at work on the 39th floor of Denver's 56-story Republic Plaza. Completed in 1984, Colorado's tallest building boasts 1,200,000 square feet of office space and 55,000 square feet of shops.
Photographer:
Alan Berner, USA

• *Right*

Aerobics are the lunch-time fare on the roof of the downtown International Athletic Club in health-conscious Denver, Colorado.
Photographer:
Alan Berner, USA

Left

First graders Stephanie Barrowman and Meghan Courtney share a secret outside Apollo Elementary School in Titusville, Florida. The school opened 19 years ago when the Apollo Lunar Program was operating full tilt at nearby Kennedy Space Center. Roughly half the school's students have at least one parent who works for NASA or related private companies.

Photographer:

Penny Tweedie, Britain

Children see the world with fresh eyes. On Friday, May 2nd, Kodak supplied two hundred American school children with Kodak Disc Cameras. In return for working on *A Day in the Life of America*, the children were allowed to keep their cameras. On this page is a selection from the 9,600 photographs shot by this army of young photographers.

Dennis Towne, Age 13 **Manti, Utah**

Misty Colvin, Age 12 **Riggins, Idaho**

Nettie Ann Alvarez, Age 10 **Denver, Colorado**

Brian McAdam, Age 8 **Littleton, Colorado**

Misty Colvin, Age 12 **Riggins, Idaho**

Douglas Kacena, Age 10 **Littleton, Colorado**

Gwyneth Campbell, Age 13 — Lakewood, Colorado

Sarah Cook, Age 9 — Englewood, Colorado

Jason Scott Smith, Age 10 — Jeffersonville, Indiana

Theo Bush, Age 7 — Denver, Colorado

Bevin Carithers, Age 12 — Arvada, Colorado

Sky Patterson, Age 8 — San Antonio, Texas

● *Above, top*

A photo-collage by graduating senior Alexander Frankfurter attracts attention at the Rhode Island School of Design's Woods-Gerry Gallery in Providence.

Photographer:
Gianfranco Gorgoni, Italy

● *Above*

On the set of his latest film at Astoria Studios in Queens, New York, director Woody Allen lines up a shot with cinematographer Carlo DiPalma.

Photographer:
Steve McCurry, USA

Below

"Linda," a 1983 work by hometown sculptor John DeAndrea, is one of the big draws at the Denver Art Museum. The stunningly lifelike effect was achieved by making a vinyl mold of model Linda Keller.

Photographer:
Alan Berner, USA

Following page

The weekly baptism ceremony at the Heritage Grand Hotel in Fort Mill, South Carolina. The hotel is a part of Heritage, USA, a Christian community headed by television evangelists Jim and Tammy Bakker.

Photographer:
Jerry Valente, USA

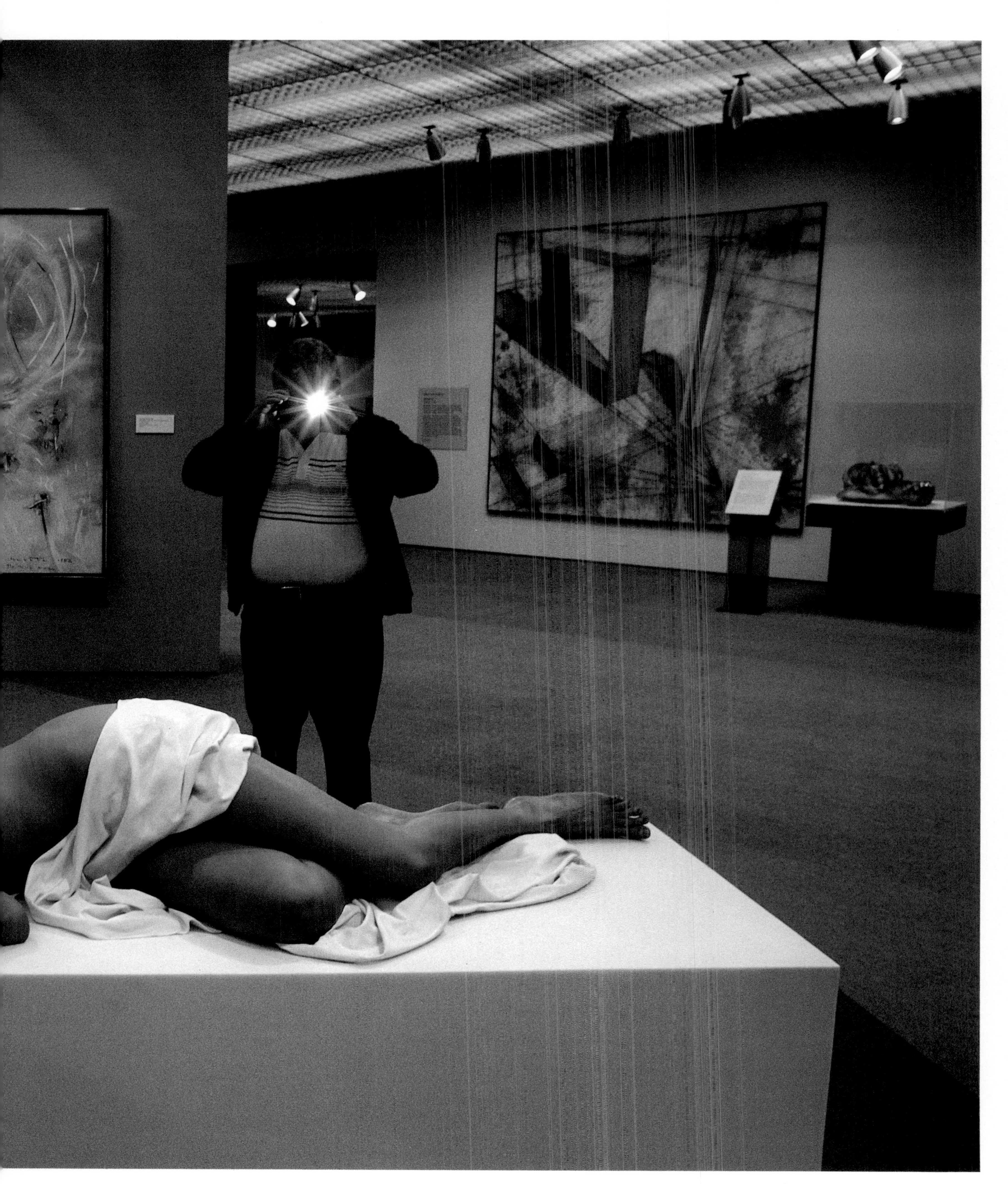

Jerry Valente

Hair Stylist

Left

A basic wash, cut and dry costs $40 at Carlo Manfredi's Hairpower on Manhattan's St. Mark's Place. Hairpower is open from 10 a.m. to midnight seven days a week. Like many East Village shopowners, Manfredi is being forced out after 16 years by a fivefold rent increase—to $10,000 a month for his 500-square-foot shop.
Photographer:
Steve McCurry, USA

Above

Housewife Edna Lautenschlager under the dryer at Georgetta's Styling Salon in Palmer, Nebraska (population: 450). Owner Georgetta Platt charges $10 for a wash, cut and dry.
Photographer:
Maddy Miller, USA

• *Above*

In January 1984, Martin Carrillo, 30, joined the more than 2,700 convicts doing time in the Texas state prison system for a drug offense (in his case, possession of heroin, in El Paso). Carrillo's maximum sentence of six years is just over half the state-wide average for new inmates.
Photographer:
Ethan Hoffman, USA

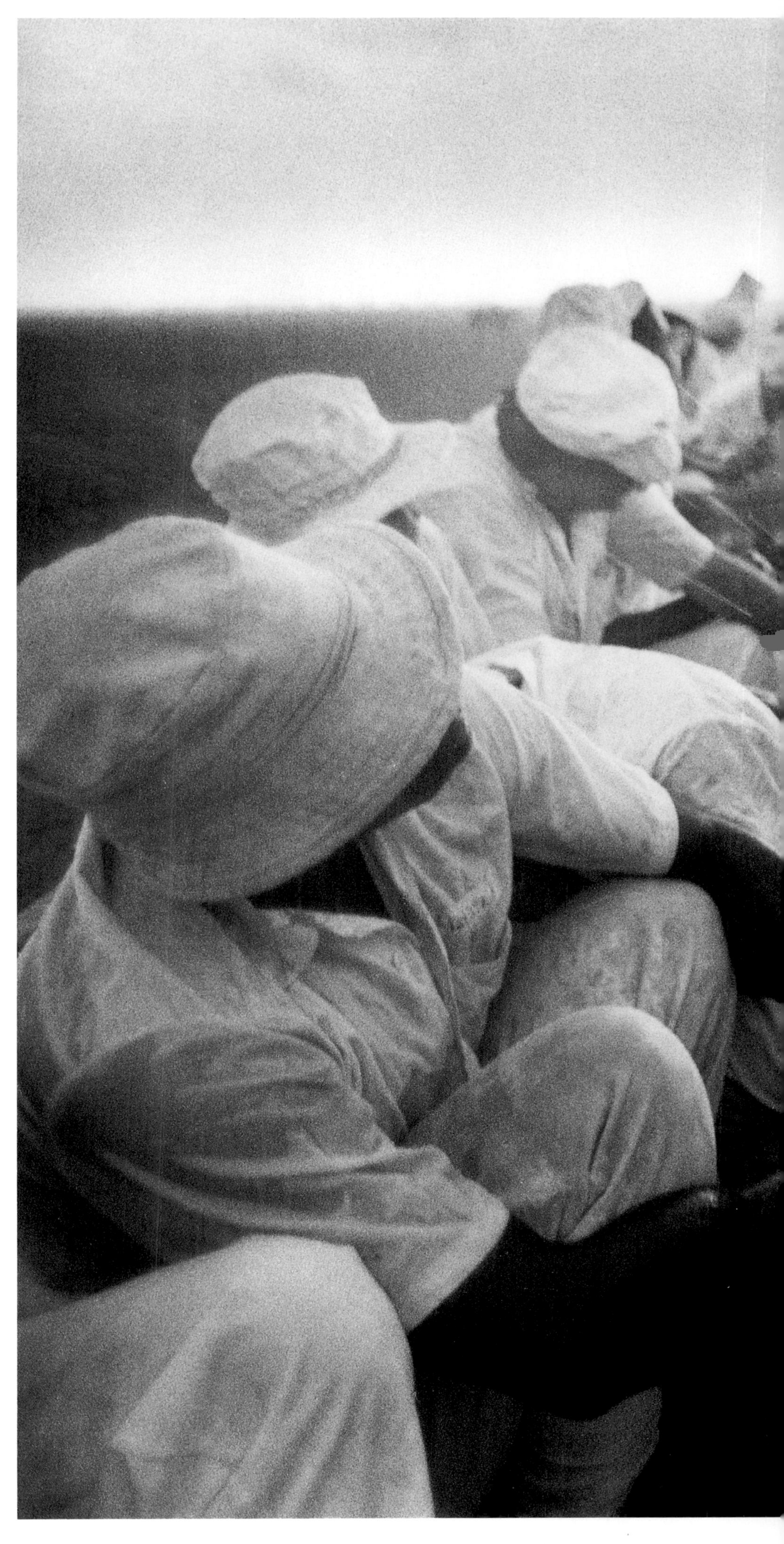

• *Right*

Ramsey Units I, II and III of the Texas Department of Corrections house more than 3,500 inmates—nearly a tenth of the state's total prison population—on an 18,000-acre farm near Angleton, Texas. Squads of 25 to 30 prisoners work eight hours a day, five days a week at Ramsey's agricultural operation. On May 2nd, this group waited in a driving rainstorm for more than an hour while guards chased down—and eventually caught—a prisoner who tried to escape.
Photographer:
Ethan Hoffman, USA

Life is just a fantasy for Siegfried & Roy, the German-born "master illusionists" whose stage spectacular, *Beyond Belief,* has been headlining at Las Vegas' Frontier Hotel since 1981. On May 2nd, *Day in the Life of America* photographer Francois Robert visited "the Wizards of Joy" at their nearby $10 million home, "Jungle Palace," where the attractions included two rare white tigers (white with black stripes), an even rarer snow white tiger (completely white with ice blue eyes), and a fancy bit of levitation.

Robert (pronounced *row-bear*) says, "After a long negotiation with their manager, we arrived at Siegfried & Roy's well-protected mansion and were admitted along with a local television news crew. I wanted to shoot the levitation over water, and, being master showmen, they agreed to do it in the tiger pen. As we discussed earlier, I set up my cameras and then left the scene. When they called us back 25 minutes later, Roy was already levitating. I never found out how they did it, but in a way, I'm glad. I'd rather believe there's still some magic in the world."

Photographer:
Francois Robert, Switzerland

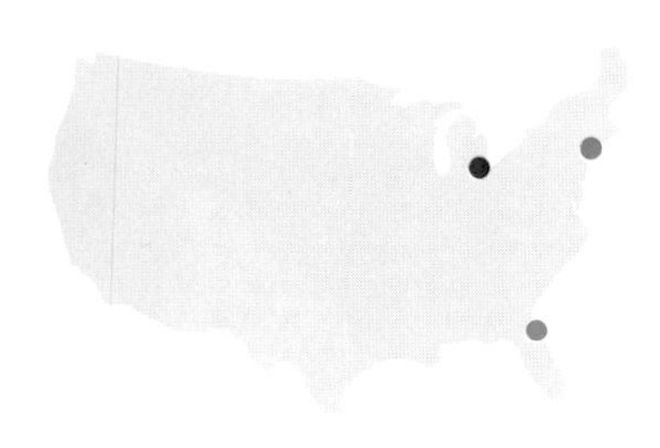

THIS IS THE SECOND ARK
AND
THIS IS A JUDGMENT SIGN
PREPARE YOURSELF TO MEET YOUR GOD

Left, top

Amooh Saleh, an immigrant from Yemen, prays toward Mecca in the living room of her Dearborn, Michigan home.

Photographer:
Anthony Suau, USA

Left, bottom

Mother Superior Essie Mae McDonald at the Mt. Zion, Overcoming Body of Christ, the True Bride Church in Crescent City, Florida. "Our message is universal," she says, "and we send it out—love, peace and joy in the world."

Photographer:
Wally McNamee, USA

Below

Pastor Lorenzo Pettway leads a "deliverance service"—including gospel singing, prayer, testimonials and Scripture readings—at the Household of Faith Holy Ghost Deliverance Church in Bridgeport, Connecticut. Founded in a storefront in 1981, the congregation was more than 200 strong on May 2, 1986.

Photographer:
Daniel Lainé, France

● *Above*

Frank and Margery Brown of Chelsea, Vermont, are members of the Ed Larkin Contra Dancers. On May 2nd, they showed their stuff in Chelsea Town Hall. Contra dancing is a type of square dancing, done in lines instead of squares. The 40-member group—named for fiddle player Ed Larkin who started the group in 1934—has about 40 regular members with an average age of 69.

Photographer:
Christopher Pillitz, Britain

● *Right*

B. T. (''Bennie'') Wrinkle, 85, cares full-time for his wife, Minnie, confined by strokes and heart trouble to a hospital bed in their living room. Wrinkle still grows vegetables and churns his own butter on a farm his grandfather started a century ago in Lebanon, Missouri.

Photographer:
Patrick Tehan, USA

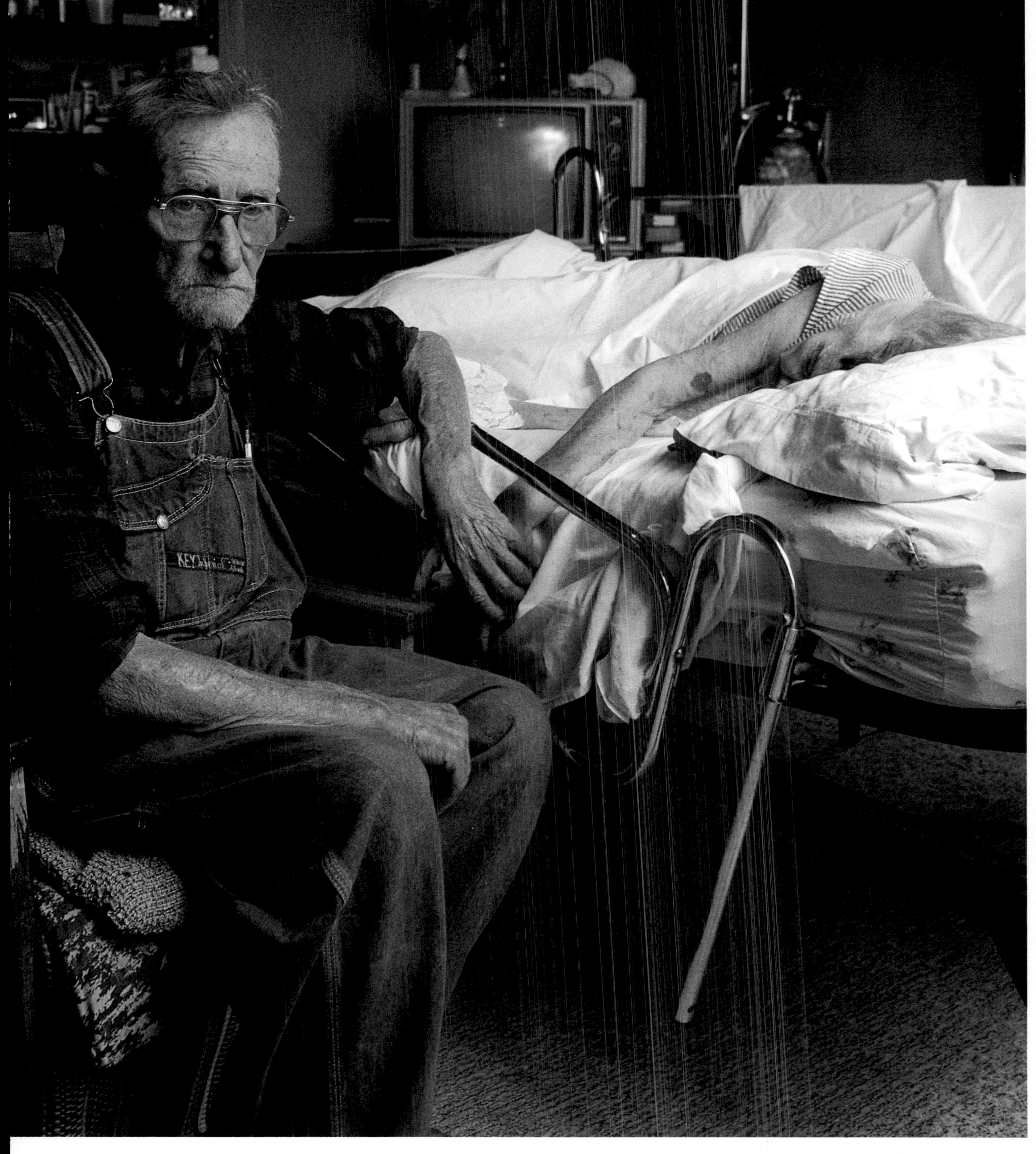

● *Left*

She used to bring a hymnal, but now this true believer brings her "box" to record a live gospel music performance outside Reverend Tim Hicks trailer church in Soperton, Georgia.
Photographer:
Tomasz Tomaszewski, Poland

● *Above*

They used to call it recess, but in 1986, it's "physical development time" for 130 kids age two through six at the Palo Alto Preschool Center in Glendale, Arizona.
Photographer:
Andy Hernandez, Philippines

● *Following page*

Big bucks: Elaina Britton, 5, comes face to face with Alexander Hamilton of ten-dollar-bill fame at the Great American Marketplace exhibit in Oklahoma City's Enterprise Square.
Photographer:
Daniel Aubry, USA

Daniel Aubry

J 13008303 A
UNITED STATES OF AMERICA
TWO DOLLARS
J 67811325 E
FEDERAL RESERVE NOTE
UNITED STATES OF AMERICA
A 65036466 B
WASHINGTON, D.C.
TEN DOLLARS
A special seminar has been announced for grocery store owners to consider new ways to increase sales. The sessions will be conducted by Lee Warren Boswell who has spent many years in the food business.
The meetings will be held in the Civic Center at Lakeland, Florida, on September 8 and 9 starting at 9 a.m.
Those interested in attending the meetings should write the Florida Grocery Association, 30 North Iowa Ave., Lakeland, Florida, for more information.

• *Above*

Textile workers head home after the early shift (7 a.m. to 3 p.m.) at the Fieldcrest Cannon sheet and towel mill in Kannapolis, North Carolina.
Photographer:
Peter Turnley, USA

• *Right*

Clerk Matthew Barrall contemplates the ruins of a rough day in the trading pits at the Chicago Options Exchange where a total of 438,000 contracts changed hands on May 2nd.
Photographer:
Paul Chesley, USA

Letizia Battaglia

Volker Hinz

New Ulm, Minnesota

Flip Schulke

Gainesville, Georgia

Gerrit Fokkema

Eugene, Oregon

Gianni Giansanti

Reno, Nevada
Dana Fineman

Savannah, Georgia
Gerd Ludwig

Baltimore, Maryland
Luc Choquer

Arthur Grace

• Previous page

Amy Foote and Paul Neis are regular exercise partners at the Monday, Wednesday and Friday aerobics class at the San Mateo Nautilus Fitness Center in Albuquerque, New Mexico.
Photographer:
Arthur Grace, USA

• Right

Giovanni Rigato, his wife, Mary, and their daughters Bridget, 9 (center), and Elena, 10, in front of their row house on Albemare Street in the ''Little Italy'' section of East Baltimore. (Sister-in-law Bernadette Quinn and her two-year-old daughter Maria are on the steps.)

Rigato came to the United States from Bolzano in 1970 and now owns Capriccio Restaurant, around the corner on Fawn Street. The girls are wearing uniforms from nearby St. Stanislaus School. ''Little Italy,'' a 12-block area near Baltimore's Inner Harbor, is one of the city's 237 identifiable neighborhoods.
Photographer:
Luc Choquer, France

D. Gorton

● *Previous page*

Mrs. Robert Stott is a sponsor of the prestigious Delta Debutante Club. On May 2nd she held afternoon tea lessons on the veranda of the Retzer home in Greenville, Mississippi. The young ladies on the left are "pages," age 12 and 13, who attend the debutantes at balls and dream of the day when they, too, will turn 18. The younger ladies to the right, age eight to ten, are called "little friends."

Photographer:

D. Gorton, USA

● *Left*

New York City real estate czar Donald Trump planted 21 eleven-foot Bradford pear trees on the terraces of his gilded Fifth Avenue showcase, Trump Tower.

Photographer:

Jodi Cobb, USA

● *Above*

Lt. Mark J. Kerski applies an official "bust" sticker to the 110-foot U.S. Coast Guard vessel *Sea Hawk* in its home port of Key West, Florida. Each leaf symbol represents a marijuana seizure, and each snowflake, a cocaine seizure. Between 1972 and May 1986, the U.S. Coast Guard intercepted over 25 million pounds of marijuana and 10,000 pounds of cocaine—probably a small fraction of the illegal drugs that entered the United States during that period.

Photographer:

Robb Kendrick, USA

● *Below*

Melvin Red Cloud, great-grandson of the famous Sioux chief, paints grave markers in the carpenter's shop at Pine Ridge's Holy Rosary Mission, run by the Jesuits. The crosses will mark previously unmarked graves at the Oglala town cemetery.

Don Doll is chairman of the visual and performing arts department at Creighton University, an active photojournalist and a Jesuit priest. For the past ten years, he has documented the life and times of the Sioux Indians on South Dakota reservations. On May 2nd, Doll returned to South Dakota to photograph a day in the life of the Pine Ridge Reservation.

Photographer Doll says, "When I saw Melvin, I was reminded of all the friends I have lost to alcoholism, violence and suicide."

Photographer:
Don Doll, S.J., USA

● *Above, top*

Robin Thunder Horse, 20, and Charles Alcott, 17, at home with their two-week-old son, Corey. Alcott, who is half Navajo and half Sioux, is a junior at Red Cloud High School. Thunder Horse stays home with Corey. In the background is housemate Marlette Yellow Horse with her children.

Photographer:
Don Doll, S.J., USA

● *Above*

Robert Fast Horse, chief tribal judge, in his chambers at the tribal courthouse in Pine Ridge, South Dakota. Fast Horse, a graduate of the University of New Mexico School of Law, makes his rulings in accordance with the Oglala Sioux Tribe Law and Order Code, drafted by the tribal council.

Photographer:
Don Doll, S.J., USA

● *Right*

At the Vietnam War Memorial in Washington, D.C., Vietnam veteran Gary Wright Jr. of McLean, Virginia, gives his son Gary III a boost to kiss the name of his grandfather, Col. Gary G. Wright Sr., who was killed in action.

Photographer:

Seny Norasingh, Laos

Dave Shippee

● *Previous page*

Basque sheepherder Francisco Lezamiz tends a band of approximately 2,300 sheep in the hills outside Emmett, Idaho. Lezamiz, who works for the Highland Livestock and Land Company of Emmett, spends nine months of the year camping out with the animals. He came to America from northern Spain in 1972 and is one of over 4,000 Basques who reside in Idaho—many of whom work as sheepherders.

Photography contest winner.

Dave Shippee, USA

● *Left*

On May 2nd, Americans were preparing for the upcoming Statue of Liberty Centennial Celebration. Photographer Dilip Mehta encountered the refurbished 225-ton, 152-foot-high lady in a striking late afternoon light.

Photographer:

Dilip Mehta, Canada

● *Above*

Marvin Williams (left) and Marvin Stevens, maintenance men, cleaning up at the Paramus Park Shopping Center in Paramus, New Jersey.

Photographer:

Diego Goldberg, Argentina

U.S. AIR FORCE T-38A NO-
A.F. SERIAL NO.
65-10325
SERVICE THIS AIRCRAFT WITH GRADE
JP-4 FUEL. IF NOT AVAILABLE, T.O. NO
WILL BE CONSULTED FOR
EMERGENCY ACTION
SUITABLE FOR USE OF AROMATIC FUEL
1. PUSH LATCH
2. PULL "D" HAN
TO JETTISON
WARNING
THIS AIRPLANE CONTAINS
CANOPY REMOVERS CONTAINING
EXPLOSIVE CHARGES. SEE APPLIC
-2 AIRCRAFT T.O. FOR COMPLE
INSTRUCTIONS
STATIC PORT
U.S. AIR F
STEP
STEP
FWD

● *Left*

Airman First Class Mark Nowotny, a 26-year-old maintenance specialist, washes the canopy of a T-38A advanced jet trainer used by student test pilots at Edwards Air Force Base, home of "the right stuff."
Photographer:
Roger Ressmeyer, USA

● *Above*

The Space Rocket Center of Huntsville, Alabama, operates the United States Space Camp, where children ages 10-15 spend a week learning the basics of space travel. Here, Tony Gardner lends a helping hand to fellow camper Christian Conte.
Photographer:
Debra Schulke, USA

Hot young fashion photographer Sante D'Orazio was born and raised in Brooklyn. Model Kristen McMenamy grew up in Allentown, Pennsylvania, and began her professional career in New York in November 1984. On May 2nd, they worked together on a Manhattan rooftop shooting an ad for a European lingerie company.

Burk Uzzle, who photographed this rooftop scene, chose his shooting technique very carefully. He says, "My assignment was to shoot the fashion industry backstage, the flip side of the slick fashion photographs that we all see on the cover of *Vogue*. I did all my shooting in black and white to separate my shots very quickly from ordinary fashion photos. I also decided to use a wide angle lens almost all the time in order to show these people in context and to give the viewer an idea of the extraordinary things the photographer and model go through to get glamorous pictures."

Photographer:
Burk Uzzle, USA

The *Day in the Life* sponsors and *Popular Photography* magazine issued a challenge to photographers: "Dust off your cameras on May 2nd and match your photographic skills against 200 of the world's top photojournalists." A host of talented photographers accepted the challenge and entered their best efforts in the *Day in the Life of America* photography contest. Some of the entries are seen on this page. Others appear throughout the book.

Jockey's Ridge, Outer Banks, North Carolina — Henry Stindt

Braddock, Pennsylvania — Jack McKenzie

Cambridge, Massachusetts — Elizabeth Wilson

Maui, Hawaii — Sherry Lee Thompson

Washington, D.C. — William E. Woolam

Erie, Pennsylvania — Diane R. McCafferty

Houston, Texas — Rob Muir

New York, New York — Shaun Considine

New Vienna, Iowa — Julie Habel

Houston, Texas — Rob Muir

Pace, Mississippi — Jeff McAdory

Line Creek, Wyoming — Mark A. Payler

● *Below*

Bob Montgomery, a Washington, D.C., law student, dives into the rooftop pool at the Eldorado Hotel in Santa Fe, New Mexico.
Photographer:
Arnaud de Wildenberg, France

● *Right, top*

Florida "mermaids" suit up for an underwater extravaganza at Weeki Wachee Spring near Orlando.
Photographer:
Misha Erwitt, USA

● *Right, bottom*

A trainer takes time out for a trick with one of his charges at the Dolphin Research Lab in Marathon, Florida.
Photographer:
Jennifer Erwitt, USA

5:45 PM

Mayor George Ahmaogak Sr. presides over Alaska's North Slope Borough, an 80,000-square-mile expanse of ice and tundra that includes the town of Barrow, seven smaller villages and 20% of America's daily oil production. Ahmaogak—like 80% of his 8,300 constituents—is an Iñupiat Eskimo, one of Alaska's original inhabitants. Each spring, Ahmaogak heads out to hunt whales the old-fashioned way, through breaks in the Arctic Ocean ice pack.

All 200 *Day in the Life of America* photographers were asked to make a portrait of the mayor of the town or city where they were assigned. Photographer Jim Balog made this shot of Mayor Ahmaogak eight miles out on the ice pack off Barrow, Alaska. Other *Day in the Life* photographers worked in more temperate surroundings, photographing hizzoners ranging from New York's flamboyant Edward Koch to Cuba, Kansas' Steve Benyshek. Photographer D. Gorton, however, found the only mayor, male or female, who wanted to pose in ballet tights and a tutu, Greenville, Mississippi's William C. Burnley Jr. To meet a sampling of America's mayors, please turn the page.

Photographer:
James Balog, USA

Jim Richardson

Steve Benyshek
Cuba, Kansas

Michael Melford

Ace Barton
Riggins, Idaho

P.F. Bentley

Andrew Young
Atlanta, Georgia

Robb Kendrick

Tom Sawyer
Key West, Florida

Chris Johns

Pawnee Bill Smith
Hooverville, Kansas

Mike Abrahams

Tom Kough
Austin, Minnesota

John Giannini

Mary Anderson
Kinney, Minnesota

Yann Arthus-Bertrand

Sonny Scalese
Sunburst, Montana

John Giannini

Richard Nordvold
Hibbing, Minnesota

Dennis Chamberlin

Robert Kozaren
Hamtramck, Michigan

Patrick Tehan

Howard Johnson
Buffalo, Missouri

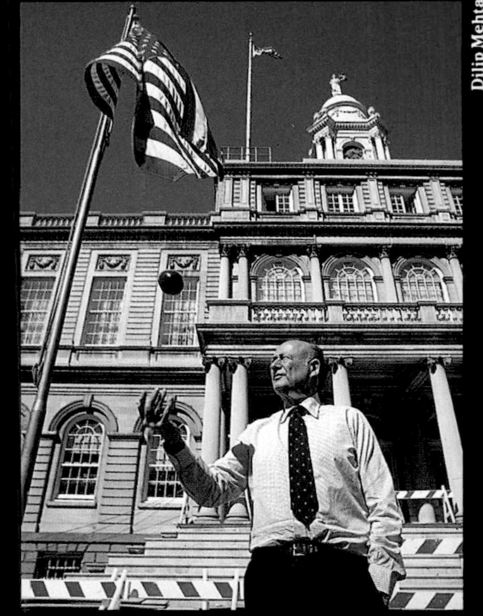

Dilip Mehta

Edward Koch
New York City, New York

Graeme Outerbridge

Page Worth
Belfast, Maine

Sara Krulwich

Cesar Dabdoub Chavez and Marcelino Varona
Nogales Sonora, Mexico and Nogales, Arizona

Andy Nelson

Kenneth Henke Jr.
Keokuk, Iowa

Tomasz Tomaszewski

Frank Radford
Soperton, Georgia

D. Gorton

William C. Burnley Jr.
Greenville, Mississippi

Yan Morvan

Dianne Feinstein
San Francisco, California

GENUINE

● *Left*

In Sacramento, California, Jerry McCarthy and Renee Jenkins warm up for an evening concert featuring country-rock band Alabama.

Photographer:

Susan Biddle, USA

● *Above*

Linda Scalese, 18, shows off her wedding dress to best friends Patricia Kimmet and Keri Alstad in her bedroom in Sunburst, Montana.

Photographer:

Yann Arthus-Bertrand, France

● *Right*

Paul Mello, a 23-year-old marine electrician, wanted his girlfriend's name inscribed on his shoulder in Chinese. On May 2nd, Buddy's Tattoo Shop in Newport, Rhode Island (''The Very Best in Tattooing, Since 1948. Individual Needles & Colours for Each Customer''), obliged. Buddy, who is also responsible for the dragon, got the proper Chinese characters—or at least a close approximation—from a waiter at a nearby Chinese restaurant.

Photographer:
Michael O'Brien, USA

The

Two men assault a drunk in an alley off Winston Street in downtown Los Angeles, an area better known as "Skid Row." *Day in the Life of America* photographer Sarah Leen says, "I turned into an alley and saw a mugging down at the end of the block. My first instinct was, Can I change my lens fast enough? I stood there, and I photographed the whole incident, then the muggers started running up the alley toward me, and I quickly turned around so they couldn't see my cameras. But they just blew right by me and disappeared. I thought maybe I was shaking too much for the picture to come out."

Photographer:
Sarah Leen, USA

Savannah Highway, Charleston, South Carolina

Aaron Chang, US

Highway 17, Charleston, South Carolina

Aaron Chang, USA

Patrick Ward

Previous page
Below
PIT-N-PATIO

Michael O'Brien

● *Previous page*

On May 2nd, air traffic controllers monitored over 2,200 takeoffs and landings at Chicago's O'Hare, the world's busiest airport.
Photographer:
Paul Chesley, USA

● *Below*

The Clover Grill at the corner of Bourbon and Dumaine in New Orleans' French Quarter closes for only four hours a year—to clean up after Mardi Gras revelers. Owner Tom Wood parks his prized Cadillac right outside.
Photographer:
David Alan Harvey, USA

● *Following page*

The San Francisco Bay Bridge carries evening commuters out of the city to Oakland, Berkeley and points east.
Photographer:
Rick Smolan, USA

NO STOPPING
8AM TO NOON
WED & SAT
STREET
CLEANING
TOW AWAY
ZONE
741
7AM - 7PM

Rick Smolan

• *Left and above*

Despite a judge's orders, the Ku Klux Klan in Gainesville, Georgia, has taken to marching on mostly black sections of town in full regalia—ostensibly to protest the sale of drugs. Most folks around Gainesville are embarrassed about the Klan's recent resurgence. City Manager Ray Keith says succinctly, "We don't appreciate or need this type of activity in our city."

Retired poultry inspector Elizabeth Carey, seen at left with her 16-month-old great-granddaughter, Brandy Rowden, says she joined the Klan to fight "drug addiction and abortion clinics." But the big and rather more ominous draw still seems to be old-fashioned cross-burnings, like this one on May 2nd in a Gainesville Klansman's backyard.

Photographer:
Gerrit Fokkema, Australia

● *Right*

On May 2, 1986, America was worried about atomic fallout from the April 26th meltdown at the Chernobyl nuclear reactor in the Soviet Union. Meanwhile, at least part of the Three Mile Island nuclear power plant—site of America's own worst nuclear malfunction in 1979—was once again operating full steam ahead.

Three Mile Island's Unit 1 was reopened in October 1985, within 24 hours of a United States Supreme Court decision permitting its operation. To the left of its twin cooling towers stands ill-fated TMI Unit 2, where the partial meltdown occurred. Seven years after the Three Mile Island accident, workers were still cleaning up the radioactive mess in Unit 2, while Unit 1 was turning six pounds of enriched uranium a day into enough electricity to power 500,000 homes in eastern Pennsylvania and New Jersey.

Photographer:
Volker Hinz, West Germany

● *Above*

Prom night at the Linwood Country Club, New Jersey: 326 graduating seniors from Atlantic City High School paid $40 per couple to attend the gala event. The theme of the 1986 dance was "The Best of Times."

Photographer:

R. Ian Lloyd, Canada

Photographer Mary Ellen Mark shot 70 rolls of film on May 2nd, 11 in color and 59 black and white. Reproduced below is one of her contact sheets—(all of the images are from one roll of film)—showing the Gibbs Senior High School prom in St. Petersburg, Florida. Which photograph would you have selected for *A Day in the Life of America*? To see which frame the picture editors finally chose, please turn to the next page.

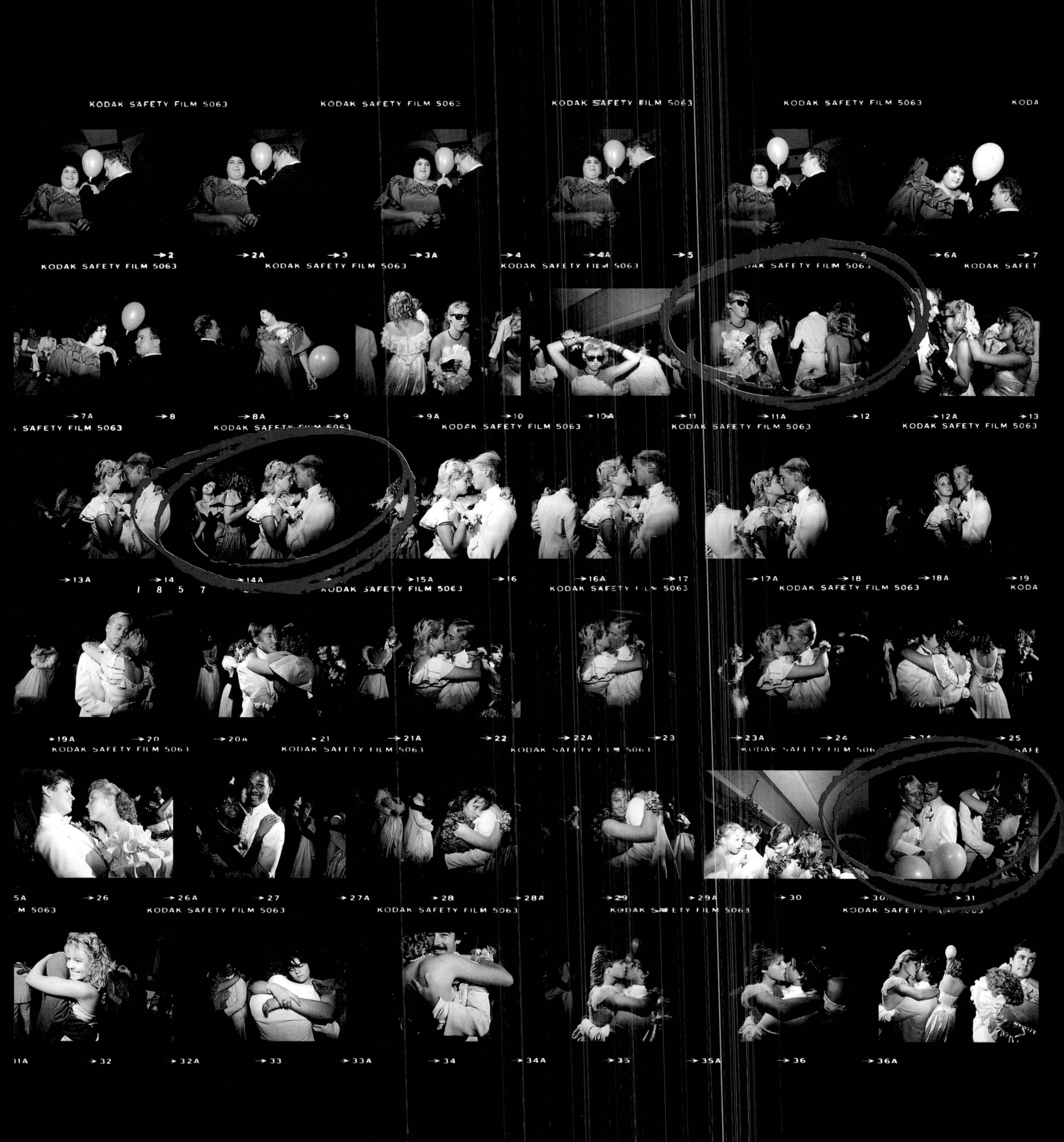

Chris Johns

DOUBLE YOUR MONEY
BACK GUARANTEE
$4.88
$2.18

● *Left*

"Smokey's Greatest Shows" brings a dozen rides and other attractions to Millinocket, Maine, each year in early May, courtesy of the local Elks club. "I shot in the Arctic for *A Day in the Life of Canada*, and the conditions were similar shooting this picture," says photographer Sam Garcia. "It was 29 degrees with a 30-mile-an-hour wind, but the carnival went on anyway."

Photographer:
Sam Garcia, USA

● *Above, top*

Stuart Parker, 24, and Robin Ritchie, 26, watch one of 1986's comedy hits, "Down and Out in Beverly Hills," at the Gem Theater in Kannapolis, North Carolina—the only show in town and one of the country's few remaining $1 movie houses.

Photographer:
Peter Turnley, USA

● *Above*

At the Beer Barn Drive Thru at the corner of Park Lane and Greenville Avenue in Dallas, you can buy beer, wine and light snacks without ever leaving your car. On a good weekend, the Beer Barn moves upwards of 150 16-gallon kegs of beer. Budweiser is most popular, Coors Lite a strong second.

Photographer:
Barry Lewis, Britain

Photographers' Assignment Locations

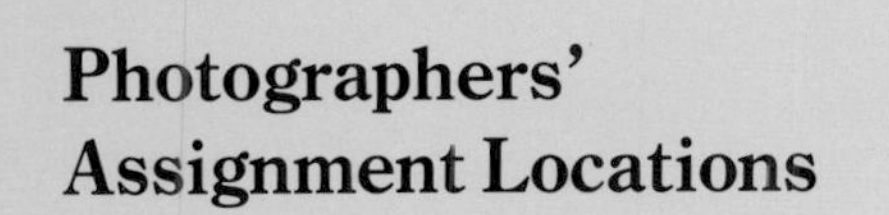

On May 2, 1986, United Airlines flew the 200 *Day in the Life* photographers listed below to their assigned locations. Our special thanks to United, the only airline serving all 50 states and therefore the only airline able to take on a project of this scope.

1 Joe Abell
2 Sam Abell
3 Mike Abrahams
4 Yuri Abramochkin
5 Eddie Adams
6 William Albert Allard
7 Yann Arthus-Bertrand
8 James K.W. Atherton
9 Daniel Aubry
10 José Azel
11 Robert Azzi
12 Sen. Howard Baker
13 Eric Lars Bakke
14 James Balog
15 Micha Bar-Am
16 Nina Barnett
17 Letizia Battaglia
18 Dieter Bauer
19 Nicole Bengiveno
20 P.F. Bentley
21 Alan Berner
22 Susan Biddle
23 Alain Bizos
24 Susan Bloom
25 Koo Bohn-Chang
26 Agnes Bonnot
27 Alex Bowie
28 Torin Boyd
29 David Burnett
30 Michele Cardon
31 Dennis Chamberlin
32 Aaron Chang
33 Gary Chapman
34 Paul Chesley
35 Luc Choquer
36 Rich Clarkson
37 Jodi Cobb
38 Serge Cohen
39 Sandy Colton
40 Anne Day
41 Arnaud de Wildenberg
42 William DeKay
43 Jay Dickman
44 Pascal Dolemieux
45 Don Doll, S.J.
46 Dan Dry
47 Susan Duca
48 Stephane Duroy
49 Tsuneo Enari
50 Jennifer Erwitt
51 Misha Erwitt
52 Miguel Luis Fairbanks
53 Ben Fernandez
54 Donna Ferrato
55 Dana Fineman
56 Victor Fisher
57 Gerrit Fokkema
58 Frank Fournier
59 Roland Freeman
60 Raphaël Gaillarde
61 J. Carl Ganter
62 Sam Garcia
63 Wilbur E. Garrett
64 Yves Gellie
65 Georg Gerster
66 John Giannini
67 Gianni Giansanti
68 Diego Goldberg
69 Lynn Goldsmith
70 Gianfranco Gorgoni
71 D. Gorton
72 Philip Gould
73 Arthur Grace
74 Stormi Greener
75 Sara Grosvenor
76 Jim Gund
77 Carol Guzy
78 Skeeter Hagler
79 Al Harvey
80 David Alan Harvey
81 Gregory Heisler
82 Andy Hernandez
83 François Hers
84 Volker Hinz
85 Ethan Hoffman
86 Eikoh Hosoe
87 Françoise Huguier
88 Graciela Iturbide
89 Chris Johns
90 Lynn Johnson
91 Frank Johnston
92 Peter Jordan
93 Han Juce
94 Shelly Katz
95 Alain Keler
96 Robb Kendrick
97 David Hume Kennerly
98 Mitch Kezar
99 Douglas Kirkland
100 Sara Krulwich
101 Hiroji Kubota
102 Kaku Kurita
103 Jean-Pierre Laffont
104 Daniel Lainé
105 Xavier Lambours
106 Gov. Richard Lamm
107 Jacques Langevin
108 Brian Lanker
109 Frans Lanting
110 Sarah Leen
111 Andy Levin
112 Barry Lewis
113 R. Ian Lloyd
114 Gerd Ludwig
115 Jay Maisel
116 Pascal Maitre
117 Mary Ellen Mark
118 John Marmaras
119 Adam Mastoon
120 Stephanie Maze
121 Linda McConnell
122 Steve McCurry
123 Joe McNally
124 Wally McNamee
125 Dilip Mehta
126 Rudi Meisel
127 Michael Melford
128 Doug Menuez
129 Claus C. Meyer
130 Maddy Miller
131 Brian Milne
132 Yan Morvan
133 Carl Mydans
134 Matthew Naythons
135 Andy Nelson
136 Chris Niedenthal
137 Alain Nogues
138 Kazuyoshi Nomachi
139 Seny Norasingh
140 Koni Nordmann
141 Michael O'Brien
142 Richard Olsenius
143 Pablo Ortiz Monasterio
144 Graeme Outerbridge
145 Daniele Pellegrini
146 Mark Peters
147 Bill Pierce
148 Mario Pignata-Monti
149 Christopher Pillitz
150 Jim Preston
151 Larry Price
152 Jake Rajs
153 Eli Reed
154 Roger Ressmeyer
155 Reza
156 Jim Richardson
157 Steve Ringman
158 Sophie Ristelhueber
159 François Robert
160 Art Rogers
161 Galen Rowell
162 April Saul
163 Debra Schulke
164 Flip Schulke
165 Mike Shayegani
166 Vladimir Sichov
167 Hans Silvester
168 Bill Simpkins
169 Tom Skudra
170 Neal Slavin
171 Rick Smolan
172 Jordi Socias
173 James L. Stanfield
174 Andrew Stawicki
175 George Steinmetz
176 Peter Stocker
177 William Strode
178 Anthony Suau
179 Michel Szulc-Krzyzanowski
180 Bruce Talamon
181 Patrick Tehan
182 Tomasz Tomaszewski
183 Aaron Tomlinson
184 David Turnley
185 Peter Turnley
186 Penny Tweedie
187 Neal Ulevich
188 Burk Uzzle
189 Jerry Valente
190 John Vink
191 Patrick Ward
192 Ron Watts
193 Mark S. Wexler
194 John H. White
195 Joy Wolf
196 Adam Woolfitt
197 Michael S. Yamashita
198 Ian Yeomans
199 Franco Zecchin
200 Tom Zetterstrom

Skeeter Hagler

A cowboy on the Pitchfork Ranch in Guthrie, Texas.

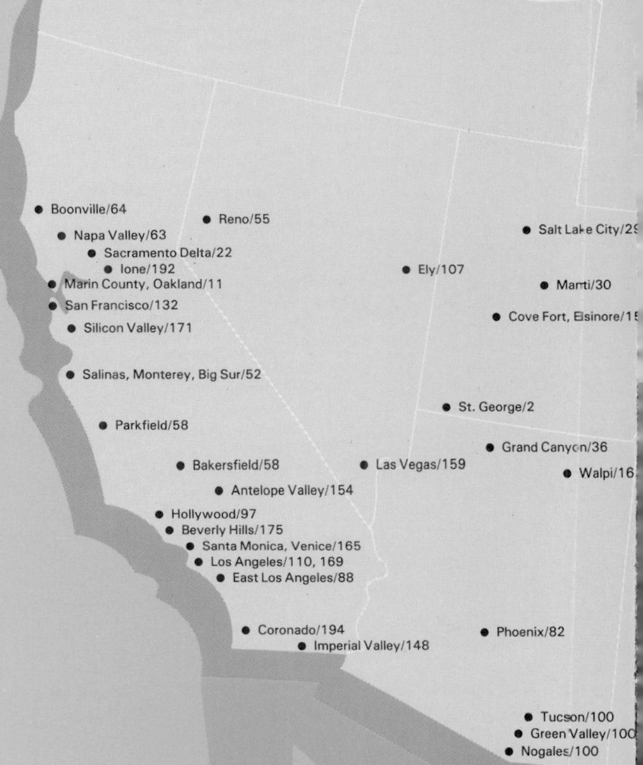

James Balog

Barrow, Alaska, the northernmost town in America.

Daniele Pellegrini

Dolly Parton greets the press before the opening of her theme park, "Dollywood," in Pigeon Fork, Tennessee.

Peter Turnley

A textile worker in Kannapolis, North Carolina.

Dan Dry

Anthony Lyvers has been curing hams for 30 years in Loretto, Kentucky.

The weather in Bermuda was lousy; in fact, tornadoes were raking the island, something that isn't supposed to happen in Bermuda. Some might have taken this as an omen. The photojournalists, in the midst of passing around a bottle or two (something their ilk is very good at), were trying to decide where to shoot next. Brazil, Italy, Ireland, China and the U.S.S.R. were all suggested, but it was the most obvious choice that the group finally settled on: It was time to bring the idea home and do America.

Smolan had his doubts. If 100 photographers were divided equally among the 50 states that would leave only two photographers to cover each state. Another problem was whether Americans would be interested in a book about the entire country—or did they just think of themselves as Californians or New Yorkers? One idea that was actually considered was to assemble 50 teams of photographers and do 51 books on the same day; one for each state and one big book with the best from all the states. Cooler heads, represented by Cohen, prevailed. "Let's just double the number of photographers to 200 and assign them according to each state's population," he suggested. In the months to come even that would prove to be a logistical nightmare.

A week after the Bermuda meeting, they called a planning session, on, as luck would have it (and they were beginning to wonder about that now), the same day as the space shuttle disaster. Among those present was Rich Clarkson, director of photography at National Geographic, who would become the director of photography for the *Day in the Life of America* (DITLA) project. To undertake the enterprise, the organizers calculated, would require the talents of no fewer than 40 staff members, a logistical team to be drawn from magazines and photo agencies all over the world. Assigning 200 photographers would entail certain logistical problems, small items such as 5000 rolls of film, 500 or so round-trip air tickets, 2000 hotel room nights, 200-plus rental cars, and maybe 20 Macintosh computers to keep track of all the etceteras. Then there was the production cost which, with top-quality, five-color printing on coated stock of a durability suitable for rafting down the Colorado River ("We want this to be on people's coffee tables 40 years from now," Smolan explained), came to a neat $4.6 million. "Hmm," they said, which was somewhat milder than the reaction of Collins Publishers, their London-based publisher.

The solution, as it had been with the other *Day in the Life* books, was to seek corporate underwriting. In all, Smolan and Cohen visited 40 companies making their pitch. "Our approach is fairly lunatic," says Cohen. "We walk into a prospective sponsor's office with 20 pounds of *Day in the Life* books under our arms and make the following offer: 'We want your company to support a photography project that takes place on one day, a day chosen because nothing special is going to happen. It's the largest such undertaking in history, and no one's ever done it before. No, we won't put any picures of your company's products in the book. No, we won't photograph your factory or your CEO. No, you can't see the book until it appears, and no, you can't censor anything. You just have to trust us and the photographers—and we can tell you in advance, the portrait you're going to get will be a warts-and-all look at the nation. What do you get in return? Your name on the first page, some free copies and the right to use duplicates of the pictures.' The wonder," Cohen smilingly adds, "is not that 34 companies turned us down, but that there were six that didn't."

With the finances in place, Smolan and Cohen flew to Europe and rounded up the heads of some of the world's leading photo agencies. Over a memorable dinner in Paris following the World Press Photo Awards, the editors, headed up by Robert Pledge, president of the New York-based picture agency, Contact Press Images, began thrashing through just who ought to take America's picture. (Another team led by *Geographic*'s Rich Clarkson was doing the same in New York.) There were, shall we say, a host of divergent opinions. But by the time the third round of cognac was quaffed everyone was feeling mellow. "It sounds corny," says Smolan, "but doing something that the experts say is impossible has a way of bringing creative people together. It's like having a common enemy."

One of their biggest enemies was time. In order to shoot the book and have it out in time for the Christmas season, the project would have to be shot in early spring, which at that point, was only two months away. The organizers also had to decide where to base themselves. Every book about America seemed to come out of the east or west coast. If they set up a base of operations in the center of the country, the book might have a different, more honest, look. The DITLA team ended up choosing Denver, Colorado on the basis of its allegedly superb air connections and lack of seductive diversions. The first allegation was true, the second, happily, was not.

The organizers also hoped that by basing themselves in Denver (rather than cynical San Francisco or jaded New York), the local community would take the project to heart. In fact, within days of their arrival, Dick Fleming, head of a downtown Denver business consortium, convinced the local movers-and-shakers that it would be "interesting" to host 200 lensmen from the far corners of the earth. The business community treated the *Day in the Life* staff with

Eric Lars Bakke

The A-Team: The Denver-based DITLA core staff included (clockwise from left): Cathy Quealy (finance), Susan Duca (intern), Gillian Houston (finance), Anne Romer (film traffic), Andrée Clift (office assistant), Gae McGregor (corporate relations), Rick Smolan (co-director), Spencer Reiss (Managing Editor), David Cohen (co-director), Curt Sanburn (assignment editor), Jennifer Erwitt (production), Patti Richards (publicity), Catherine Pledge (logistics), Amy Janello (editorial), Adam Mastoon (intern), and Torin Boyd (assignment editor). Carole Bidnick (sales) was out of town trying to sell some books.

Rich Clarkson

And if you don't like your assignment, talk to these folks. The DITLA assignment editors: (left to right, standing) Devyani Kamdar (West Coast), Jim Richardson (Northern Plains), Anne Day (New England), John Durniak (Middle Atlantic States), Sara Grosvenor (Upper South), Torin Boyd (Midwest), Victor Fisher (Middle Atlantic States), Shelly Katz (Southwest); (seated) Frank Johnston (Upper South), Curt Sanburn (Mountain States), D. Gorton (Deep South), Pam Abramson (West Coast), Spencer Reiss (Managing Editor).

more hospitality than they were used to, offering the free use of luxurious office space, cars, hotel rooms, meals, mobile telephones and even some local school buses to transport photographers around town.

The DITLA offices, meanwhile, were beginning to crowd with the first of what would eventually become hundreds of employees and volunteers. Now the tricky part began: convincing the 200 designated photographers that they should drop everything they were doing and join in this extravagant whimsy.

To understand how such a thing might have been contemplated, you have to know a little about photojournalists. They are, to put it gently, somewhat different from normal people. Their identifying marks, as those who have worked with them will testify, are a childlike curiosity (a fact, some would say, that derives from a stubborn refusal to grow up); a teenager's permanent pout ("Why can't I have my helicopter?"); a masochist's propensity for putting themselves in harm's way (who else would think of Beirut as a great place to spend a month?); and, among a tortured myriad of other characteristics, many endearing, a few not, an agoraphobe's aversion to working in packs, the photojournalists' term for which is unprintable in this context. There is, though, one susceptibility in these shy egomaniacs' Nikon-laden psyches: they love challenges. Would they abandon careers and assorted loved ones to come to the largest, most outlandish photo undertaking of all time? Of course they would.

The task of converting this presumption into reality was left chivalrously, as were the other chores deemed impossible by Messrs. Smolan and Cohen, to a woman. In this instance, Catherine Pledge, who in four days of nonstop telephoning lined up the magic 200 in a total of 33 foreign countries. While Catherine was developing cauliflower ear, Cathy Quealy was managing the office, which, depending on the hour of the day, resembled either a zoo, the headquarters of a political campaign or the nerve center for the invasion of an island somewhat larger than Grenada. As an Australian who had for six years run the daily life of her country's prime minister, Cathy thought this all quite normal.

On the other hand, Gae McGregor, DITLA's corporate marketing director, was thrown completely cold into the wheedling, bartering and begging of small items like 2000 free nights of hotel room accommodations, hundreds of United Airlines' tickets (try, sometime, to arrange the schedules of 200 not-notoriously reliable people scattered around the globe, so that they will arrive at the same place, on the same day at about the same hour) and all the other items without which DITLA would have been a Smolan-Cohen pipe dream.

Every time things started to get out of control (an almost daily occurrence) someone with the right skills would show up and offer to help. One such guardian angel was Karen Bakke, a professional travel agent who masochistically offered to donate a little time after work each day. "A little time," for Karen, like most of the other volunteers, turned out to occupy most of her waking hours.

Then there was the handling of the press, which (to the staff's initial delight, then slowly growing horror) had become unexpectedly captivated by the project. Patti Richards, the project's publicity director, thought DITLA would receive a fair amount of coverage when she mailed out releases to the newspapers and television stations in the towns the photojournalists would be covering, but nothing on the scale of what ultimately emerged. CBS rang up one day and mentioned they'd be doing a piece and would be dispatching 12 crews. ABC's "20/20" made a similar announcement, adding that they'd be fielding film crews from 83 ABC affiliates. Matters began to get out of hand when WQED, the PBS station that produces the *National Geographic* television specials, offered to do an hour documentary and send along 20 film crews. And the local media had yet to be heard from. When those calls started coming, from newspapers, television stations and some radio outlets no one had ever heard of—many of them wanting to cover the people who were covering the people who were covering America—a bleary-eyed Richards groaned, "This is getting out of control. It's turning into a media circus." Which, as it turned out, was precisely the case.

Paul Chesley

Heavyweight lightboxers: These top picture editors slaved over hot lightboxes looking at a quarter of a million *Day in the Life of America* photographs. They are (left to right, top to bottom) Anne Stovell of *Time*, Robert Pledge of Contact Press Images, Shirley Le Goubin of Colorific!, film traffic coordinator Anna Romer, Claudine Maugendre of *Actuel Magazine*, Susan Vermazen of *New York Magazine*, Arnold Drapkin of *Time*, Karen Mullarkey of *Newsweek*, Sandra Eisert of *The San Jose Mercury News*, Howard Chapnick of the Black Star agency, Michael Rand of *The Sunday Times Magazine*, London, Rich Clarkson of *National Geographic*, Woody Camp of Woodfin Camp and Associates, designer Leslie Smolan of Carbone Smolan Associates, Christian Caujolle of *Liberation*, Eliane Laffont of the Sygma Agency, Dieter Steiner of *Stern* and John Durniak.

Rick Smolan

How many Pulitzer Prize winners does it take to screw in a flash bulb? Nine were on hand for *A Day in the Life of America*. They were: (standing) Larry Price of *The Philadelphia Inquirer*, Neal Ulevich of the Associated Press, Carol Guzy of *The Miami Herald*, former White House photographer David Hume Kennerly, Jay Dickman of the *Dallas Times Herald*, Bill Strode; (kneeling) Tony Suau of Black Star, Skeeter Hagler of *The Dallas Times Herald* and John White of the *Chicago Sun-Times*.

Vladimir Sichov

National exposure: *National Geographic* photographer Jodi Cobb took a break from her DITLA assignment on New York's Fifth Avenue to make a quick appearance on the *Today Show.*

William Graves

Funny, it doesn't look like Arizona: Jim Brandenburg and Kent Kobersteen of *National Geographic* missed their DITLA assignments when they were suddenly called off to the North Pole to cover a dogsled expedition. The editors never got to see what Kobersteen would have shot in Arizona, but they did get this nice shot of the boys wearing *Day in the Life of America* T-shirts at the pole.

Sudhir

There is a pose in Spanish Harlem: David Turnley spent his *Day in the Life of America* on Manhattan's 125th Street.

Out of the frying pan, into the refrigerator: After a tense morning shooting the group portrait (page 254), Jim Balog headed off to his assignment on the northern coast of Alaska.

James Balog

With shoot day only a few weeks away, the empty room behind the DITLA offices was rapidly beginning to look like the warehouse in the final scene of *Raiders of the Lost Ark*. Under the meticulous supervision of production director Jennifer Erwitt, crates of film, cooler bags, caption books, film envelopes and 200 underwater cameras were turned into individual kits for each photographer. In addition to the necessities, many of the sponsors had donated gifts and assorted paraphernalia with their names adorning them. At one point David Cohen walked into the DITLA office simultaneously sporting three caps (Kodak, Nikon, Merrill Lynch), a Banana Republic vest, a United Airlines flight jacket, a Kodak T shirt, an Apple computer note pad and an underwater Nikon camera around his neck. "Anyone think that maybe these projects are getting a little too commercial?" Cohen asked the amused staff.

Other people were keeping busy, too, and few more so than Spencer Reiss of *Newsweek*, who was doing detached duty as DITLA's managing editor. "This project," he explained, "is like a kid's connect-the-dots puzzle, with the photographers as the dots. When you draw a line between all the dots, you end up with a picture of America. The trick is putting the dots in the right place."

Doing that was the chore of DITLA's nine assignment editors, who, aided by assistant managing editor Amy Janello, on loan from American Showcase, fanned out over the country to reconnoiter the terrain. One of them, former New York Timesman D. Gorton, spent a month traversing the Deep South by car, drinking in small town bars, scouting up lonely country lanes, painstakingly mapping out the ground over which his photographers would travel ("Smelling the docks," he called it with a distinctly Mississippi twang) and, along the way, lining up accommodations so the photojournalists would have a taste of living with typical American families.

Gorton also spent his time on the road listening to his AM car radio, alert for the crackle of Americana. Driving through rural Georgia one night, he knew he'd heard the genuine article, a fiery black radio preacher named Tim Hicks. When he called the reverend at his church, explained the project and asked if he might impose on May 2nd with a photojournalist trailed by half a dozen newspaper and television reporters, the preacher told Gorton to come on ahead. "God," he said, "has sent you to me."

Whose side the Lord was really on came briefly into question when, only a few days before the photographers pulled into Denver, there was another of those omens—the Chernobyl nuclear plant exploded—and, with it, came momentary panic. "My God," said Cohen, "what if the Russians give all our photographers visas? We'll lose all of them." Fortunately, the Russians stayed Russian and the crisis passed.

Not so easily fixed were several more mundane problems, like the fact that, thanks to the unexpected arrival of a convention of neurosurgeons, Denver's hotels were solidly booked (Sheraton eventually solved that by donating to DITLA most of an entire hotel on the outskirts of town). Also, courtesy of a transatlantic screw-up, 40 French photojournalists were cooling their heels in the Orly departure lounge, *sans billet d'avion*. With a lot of oaths and late night phone calls to DITLA's Paris agent, Annie Boulat, that glitch, too, was worked out, and the clan was on its way.

As their flights arrived, the photographers were met at the airport by staff members carrying huge *Day in the Life of America* banners. (Anyone carrying a camera bag at Stapleton International airport in Denver was assumed by the staff to be a DITLA photographer—an assumption which led to some embarassing scenes.) For the next few days, before they headed off to their assignments, the photographers would be briefed on their assignments, outfitted with their film and other paraphernalia and scared silly by the awesome competition. On the final evening, culminating three days of camaraderie, a game of Photon (a high-tech version of "capture the flag" where players dress in blinking space suits and run around shooting harmless laser guns at each other in a dark maze filled with mist) caused an impolitic moment when photographer Yuri Abramochkin, of the Soviet Union, was asked to captain the "red team." He accepted gracefully.

Giddy-up, comrade: Although it was a long ride from Moscow, Soviet photographer Yuri Abramochkin fit right in deep in the heart of Texas. Texas Governor Mark White declared him an honorary Texas citizen.

They shoot on horsey-back, don't they? Roland Freeman gives a budding young photographer a boost and a few tips at the Kodak Children's Workshop in Denver.

Swiss cheesecake: Francois Robert of Switzerland photographed these ladies of the night at a Las Vegas brothel.

Adams' eve: Eddie Adams took time out for a quick interview with the *NBC Evening News* during his assignment in Telluride, Colorado.

The next morning, before the photographers boarded planes to their assignments, John Durniak, former picture editor of *The New York Times*, gave them a last pep talk. "Friday is May 2nd," he intoned. "Shoot the hell out of the country."

Shoot the hell out of it they did, with, as you have witnessed, astounding results. Which brings us back to that question: "How did they get those shots?"

At the risk of disturbing some of the magic, the answer was a trifle more involved than being in the right place at the right time with the right light and lens opening—though, certainly, that didn't hurt.

There were, in the first place, some technical difficulties to overcome. Photojournalist Jay Dickman, for instance, found himself atop New Hampshire's Mt. Washington, site of some of the worst weather in the world, in the midst of 90 m.p.h. winds and severe sub-zero fog. That didn't bother him so much as not knowing what lens filter to use in mercury vapor lighting. A quick call to Nikon, which had set up a complete camera clinic for DITLA in Denver, straightened him out.

Nature, in the form of Idaho's Salmon River, also caused problems for Michael Melford, who spent an hour white-water rafting ("It was cold and wet, miserable; I turned blue"). In the form of high winds, it caused problems for Chris Johns, who photographed Garden City, Kansas from a crop duster. "It was kind of hairy flying," says Johns. "We were getting knocked around quite a bit. Any other day, I wouldn't have done it. But that was the job and I thought it was important to do it."

In other cases, the hazards were man-made. Australian photojournalist Gerrit Fokkema, who drew the assignment of photographing the Georgia Ku Klux Klan, turned up unannounced at the Gainesville, Georgia, home of the "Grand Titan" to find him on his front lawn, hand clutched on a pearl-handled revolver. Back-up artillery, in the form of a submachine gun, was in the house. "He said he was ready to use it," Fokkema recalls. "It was quite sobering."

In Spanish Harlem, David Turnley was accosted by an indignant resident ("A big strong guy, who looked like he was into lifting weights") with two giant Great Danes on leash. "He said I didn't belong there, and I shouldn't be taking pictures without permission," says Turnley. "He came right up to my face. His dogs were sniffing my crotch. I looked him straight in the eye and didn't back off. Finally, he drifted away. He didn't want to fight anymore than I did."

By and large, however, the DITLA photojournalists were struck by the friendliness of their subjects; indeed, of everyone they encountered. Roger Ressmeyer, who nearly had his hair singed photographing the take-off of a Mach-3, SR-71 "Blackbird" at Edwards Air Force Base, gushed, "I couldn't believe how excited people were about this project. I've been treated well before, but the Air Force and NASA people were falling all over themselves. It was like everyone was excited, almost proud, of being part of *A Day in the Life of America*. Generals were meeting me at the gate, taking me places. It was phenomenal, wonderful. I'd never experienced anything like it."

At times, the reception was so effusive the photojournalists had trouble working. Ben Fernandez, who photographed Columbus, Ohio, had his picture on the front page of the local newspaper and was trailed by fans seeking his autograph. "Instead of sneaking around quietly doing my reportage," recounts Fernandez, "I wound up being a celebrity."

No one asked Nina Barnett for her autograph, but Barnett, who covered life along the Missouri River, was also struck by American cordiality. "Usually I meet with aggression when I ask to take a person's picture," she says. "But not May 2nd. I was truly amazed how unparanoid the people were that day. They accepted me as a photographer and welcomed me into their homes. They were very proud of their lives."

Sponsors and Contributors

Major Sponsors
Eastman Kodak Company
Merrill Lynch & Co., Inc.
United Airlines
Nikon Inc.
The Hertz Corporation
Apple Computer, Inc.

Major Contributors
Banana Republic
British Airways
Brown Palace Hotel, Denver
C. W. Fentress & Associates
Cambridge Development Group
Denver Inn
Denver Public Schools
Embassy Suites Hotel, Denver
Fairmont Hotel, Denver
Holiday Inn, Denver
Image Labs
Kittredge Properties
KOA Radio 85
Marlowe's Restaurant
Marriott Hotel, Denver
Pallas Photo Lab, Inc.
Professional Travel Corp.
Radisson Hotel, Denver
Sheraton Denver Tech Center
Sill-Terhar Ford
The Burnsley Hotel, Denver
The Denver Partnership, Inc.
The Oxford Hotel, Denver

Contributors
AA/ACT, Inc.
Air France
Allright Colorado, Inc.
American Gymnastics Training Center
American Society of Magazine Photographers
Apollo Courier Systems, Inc.
ARCO Alaska
Associated Press
AT&T Information Systems
Balcar-Tekno
Bally's Park Place
Baron Aviation
Bethlehem Steel Corp.
Black Star Publishing
Boardman Youth Center
Butler Rents
Cabin Creek Health Association
Cairo Evening Citizen
California Dept. of Youth Authority
Camren Photographic Rental
CEAVCO
Center Copy
Chicago Tribune
Clarion Hotel
Cleveland Plain Dealer
Coldwell Banker Commercial Real Estate Services
Colorado National Bank of Denver
Colorado Visual Aids
Commander Submarine Force, U.S. Atlantic Fleet
Commander-in-Chief, U.S. Atlantic Fleet
Contact Press Images
Coopers & Lybrand
Copper Range Co.
Crystal Run School
Dallas Cowboys Football Club
Dallas, Texas, Police Department
Day, Webb and Taylor
Delta Queen Steam Boat Co.
Denver Art Director's Club
Denver Center for the Performing Arts
Denver Chamber of Commerce
Denver Post
Denver Public Schools
Department of the Army
Detroit Free Press
Dollywood
Dolphin Research Center
Driskell Hotel
Dworshak National Fish Hatchery
East Texas State University
Eastman Kodak Co., Denver
Eastman School of Music
Edgewater Office Products
Elliott School
Esalen, Big Sur
Esquire Magazine
Executive Helicopter
FBI School at Quantico
Federal Express Corp.
Fenn Art Galleries
Fieldcrest-Cannon Mills, Inc.
Flash Video Productions
Ford Motors
Frontier Nursing Service
Gallaudet College
General Motors
Gilchrist Lumber Co.
Graceland
GranTree Furniture Rental Corp.
Great Smokies National Park
Havey Productions
Hickory Grove Pork Farm
Hidden Valleys
Hyatt Regency Hotel
Immigration & Naturalization Services-Border Patrol
International Center of Photography
John Chalmer's Farm
K.C.H., Inc.
Kemper Military School and College
Ken Hansen Photographic, Inc.
Ken Lieberman Laboratories
Kohala Coast Resort Association
La Posada Hotel
LaJitas Inn
LaJitas Trading Post
Lane Technical High School
Latino Youth High School
Lewiston Morning Tribune
Liberation Magazine, Paris
Liberty Universtiy
Life Magazine
Lone Wolf Bar & Cafe
Los Angeles Indian Center
Los Angeles Police Department
LTV Steel Macazine
MacUser
Magnum Photos
Marillac House
MarkAir
Marriott Hotels, Chicago
Mauna Lani Bay Hotel
McDonalds, Denver
Memphis-in-May International Festival, Inc.
Mesquite Championship Rodeo
Milwaukee Sentinel
Mischer Corp.
Mustang Ranch
NASA, Ames, A.F.B.
NASA, Edwards, A.F.B.
National Archives
National Hot Rod Association
National Park Service, U.S. Department of the Interior
Nautilus Fitness Centers of New Mexico
Saul S. Negreann, Inc.
New York Magazine
New York Stock Exchange, Inc.
Newsweek Magazine
NewVector Communications, Inc.
Nissan Motor Manufacturing Corp., U.S.A.
North Carolina School of Arts
Northrop Corp.
Norton
Ocean Reef Club
Odessa, Texas Bureau of Tourism
Office of the Governor, State of Colorado
Office of the Governor, State of Oklahoma
Office of the Governor, State of Texas
Oglebay Norton
Ohio University
OMNI Hotel
Operation PUSH
Oral Roberts University
Pabst Brewing Co.
Paramount Theatre
Parkland Hospital
Paul Werth Associates., Inc.
Peabody Hotel
Pencils
People Magazine
Petro-Canada
Photon Video Arcade
Pitchfork Ranch
Pitney Bowes, Denver
Plume Ltd.
Pontiac Motor Division
Popular Photography
Potlatch Corp.
Power Promotions
Prabhupada's Palace of Gold
Professional Business Resources, Inc.
Provine Flying Service, Inc.
RCA Records
Read-Poland Advertising
Red Fox Inn
Research Triangle Foundation
Retail Planning Associates
RJ Reynolds Tobacco Co.
RJR Nabisco, Inc.
S & W Classics
Seaworld
Silver Streak Square and Round Dancing Festival
Skyline Building Maintenance
Special Events, Inc.
Stapleton Plaza Hotel
Stern Magazine
Stock Imagery, Inc.
Stockton Post Office
Stryker Weiner Associates
Surfing Magazine
Sygma Photos
Telos Corp.
Texas Department of Correction
Texas Sesquicentennial Commission
Texas Wagon Train Association
The Citadel
The Communications Works, Inc.
The Concord Resort Hotel
The Great Peace March
The Groton School
The Honolulu Advertiser
The National Fitness Institute
The National Geographic Society
The Petroleum Club of Billings, Montana
The Spee Club
The Sunday Times (London)
The Volunteers of America
The White House
The Yellowstone Country Club
Time Magazine
Town Properties
Traverse City Record Eagle
U.S. Air Force, Edwards AFB
U.S. Coast Guard
U.S. Dept. of Energy, Hanford Nuclear Reservation
U.S. Naval Academy
U.S. Navy, Bangor Submarine Base, Bremerton
U.S. Supreme Court
U.S.S.R. Information Department
United Mine Workers of America
United Parcel Service, Rocky Mountain District
United Steelworkers
University of Houston
University of Indiana
University of Missouri
Varig Brazilian Airlines
Waites Transport, Inc.
Weyerhauser Corp., Springfield
White Water Express
Wind Waves & Wheels Surf Shop
Woodbine Corporation
Woodfin Camp Associates
WQED, Pittsburgh
Y O Ranch
YMCA of Metropolitan Denver
Youngstown Board of Education

S. Peter Lewis

Thank you to the People of America.